THE SOCIETY OF DORSET

FOUNDED JULY 7TH, 1904

'A Silver Tower Dorset Red Banner Bears'

President:
LORD FELLOWES OF WEST STAFFORD, DL
Deputy Presidents:
SIR ANTHONY JOLLIFFE, GBE, DL, D.SC, D.MUS
DR. PAUL ATTERBURY, BA. FRSA
STUART ADAM

Past Presidents:
SIR FREDERICK TREVES, BART, GCVO, CB, LLD, 1904 - 1907
THOMAS HARDY, OM, LITT.D, JP, 1907 - 1909
COLONEL JOHN MOUNT BATTEN, CB, 1909 - 1911
COLONEL SIR ROBERT WILLIAMS, BART, VD, 1911 - 1913
SIR STEPHEN COLLINS, JP, 1913 - 1915
JOHN CASTLEMAN SWINBURNE-HANHAM, JP, 1915 - 1919
THE RIGHT HON. THE EARL OF SHAFTESBURY, KP, PC, GCVO, 1919 - 1922, 1924 - 1925
CAPTAIN THE RIGHT HON. F. E. GUEST, CBE, DSO, 1922 - 1924
CAPTAIN ANGUS V. HAMBRO, JP, DL, 1925-33, 1936 - 1944
LIEUT.-COL. SIR PHILIP COLFOX, BART, MC, 1933 - 1936
H.E. THE RIGHT HON. LORD LLEWELLIN, CBE, MC, TD, DL, 1944 - 1957
BRIGADIER G. M. B. PORTMAN, CB, TD, DL, 1957 - 1961
ROBERT TOM WARREN, 1962 - 1963
COLONEL SIR RICHARD GLYN, BART, OBE, TD, DL, 1964 - 1969
SIMON WINGFIELD DIGBY, MA, TD, DL, 1970 - 1984
SIR ANTHONY JOLLIFFE, GBE, DL, D.SC, D.MUS, 1984-2011

Past Hon. Secretaries:
WILLIAM WATKINS, JP, 1904 - 1925
H. LL. WATKINS, 1925 - 1937
S . H. J. DUNN, 1937 - 1940
E. G. GALE, 1940 - 1941
HARRY J. HARVEY, 1941 - 1942
F. C. H. DENNETT, AACCA, FRES, 1942 - 1961
W. T. G. PERROTT, MIWO, 1961 - 1969
J. C. R. PREWER, 1969 - 1979
G. E. HINE, FRICS, 1979 - 2004
H. C. RUSSELL, 2004 - 2021

Past Hon. Editors:
SIR NEWMAN FLOWER, 1914 - 1920
STANLEY L. GALPIN, 1920 - 1932
H. LL. WATKINS, 1935 - 1937
ASHLEY C. ROGERS, 1937 - 1950
FRANK C. H. DENNETT, 1951 - 1960
N. J. ('NAT') BYLES, 1961 - 1978
FRED LANGFORD, 1979 - 1994
GEORGE LANNING, 1995 - 2000
PETER PITMAN, 2001 - 2013
TREVOR VACHER-DEAN, 2014 - 2015
SELWYN WILLIAMS, 2016 - 2019
NICHOLAS WRIGHT, 2020 - 2023
PETER LUSH, 2023

THE

DORSET

YEAR BOOK

FOR 2024

ONE HUNDRED AND FIFTEENTH YEAR OF ISSUE

First published in Great Britain in 2023 by The Society of Dorset Men

A CIP catalogue record for this book is available from the British Library

Paperback ISBN: 978 0 901052 08 7

Edited by John Newth

Printed by Henry Ling Ltd at The Dorset Press, Dorchester, DT1 1HD

Cover photo: The fountain at Forde Abbey

Contents

Advertisers in italic

Stuart Adam

At the last meeting of the Society of Dorset Men, Stuart Adam resigned as Chairman after 24 years in the service of the members. He was appointed a Deputy President at the same time and, since no one has more cause to feel grateful for his help than I do, it perhaps falls to me to express our gratitude.

Stuart is indeed a Dorset Man. He was born in Blandford and he attended Blandford prep school before being sent away to boarding school beyond the borders of the county. This was followed by college where he obtained a diploma in Business Studies, which would come in very useful over the years. Afterwards, he joined Dorset County Council followed by Bournemouth Borough Council, where he worked in the Town Clerk's/Chief Executive's office. Having achieved senior officer status at a young age under the Chief Executive, Keith Lomas, he decided there was more to life than local government and started his own business.

Since making that decision, Stuart has been involved in various concerns around Dorset and Somerset, ranging from agriculture to retail and distribution. Stuart succeeded his father, the remarkable Roy Adam, whom I remember well, as Committee Chairman in 2008, having been Deputy Chairman for nine years previously. Remarkably, Stuart and his father have been Chairman, and in Stuart's case Deputy Chairman, of the Society of Dorset Men for a period of 48 years. For the past twenty years, latterly as President, I have very much relied on their support, and I have not been disappointed.

So, on behalf of us all, I would like to congratulate Stuart on being made a Deputy President, which is well deserved following his many years of really admirable service to the Society.

Julian Fellowes, Lord Fellowes of West Stafford DL

Characters from Victorian Dorset

Devina Symes pays tribute to three people whose example shaped her life

As a child in the 1950s, I was privileged to know some of the last of the Victorian Dorset characters and to hear stories about other characters who had died before I was born, all of whom had left a huge legacy of how to handle life with courage and humour.

Although not that far away, their traditions and daily routines were so very different from our 21st-century world. I should record the strong memories I have of them and the tales they have told me, or which have been passed down, before that link has gone.

Jane Cox, although no relation, was known as 'Granny' by our family. She was born in 1874 at Winfrith and I remember her well. Her family moved

to East Knighton when she was twelve years old. Like Thomas Hardy, due to her frail constitution Jane did not go to school until she was eight years old. Altogether her parents had a total of seven children, but all four who were born after Jane died before reaching adulthood. As an adult she became a domestic cook, eventually for a large household in Bristol. In 1909, when her mother's health failed, she moved back home to East Knighton and married Ernest Cox. The couple had three children:

Granny Cox by her well in the 1940s

Kitty Barker

Two views of the same part of East Knighton, the blacksmith's shop in the one from the 1920s (above) having been replaced by a garage by the 1940s (below). Now the Rainbow Garage, it is owned by the grandson of the blacksmith. Running off to the left in front of the garage is Blacknoll Lane, leading to the Countryman Inn (formerly the Rising Sun until the 1990s). The cottages on the right were demolished in the 1960s to allow the A352 to be widened.

Tony Seaward

Top of Knapp.

Phillis, Freda and John. In World War 1, Ernest was conscripted into the army and Jane had to raise her family and care for her father alone. Her husband was seriously injured in the war, which led to his early death in 1932. At the outset of World War 2, John enlisted into the Royal Navy, but once again fate was cruel to Jane as he was killed in action in August 1942, leaving her alone in her cottage. As a result, she took in lodgers who had connections with the army camp at Bovington.

My father, who had grown up in East Knighton, knew Granny, and when he and my mother were looking for lodgings just after World War 2, Granny took them in. By this time she was stone deaf, and how pleased she was that she could lip-read my mother. A close friendship was soon formed between the three. It was in the mid-1950s that I first met her. Later, when my parents had a council house in Weymouth, my mother and I used to visit her every week and on our way to the bus stop, Mum would buy some ham and sausages for Gran. She loved to see us and Dad, who would join us when he had finished work.

Granny only had her pension to live on but was very content. When her feet became painful with corns on her small toe, she would cut a hole in her plimsolls so that they would not press on them. To lock her door she would put a toothbrush across the latch, although in the daytime she never locked her front door. Her burglar-proof method was to scatter cigarette butts in the front of the cottage, saying that a would-be burglar would assume a man lived there and be put off from breaking in. Sometimes my father used to call on her in his lunch hour and often, before going in to see Gran, would empty her 'bucket', putting the contents in the garden. When she realised, she would gently admonish him for doing so in his smart clothes, telling him, 'I can't reward you, my son, but you will be rewarded.' Gran had a strong faith, and one day she remembered that Dad was going to call in at lunchtime and realised that she had nothing to give him for his lunch. Then, when she went to the front door, she found half a dozen eggs on the doorstep: a friend from Winfrith had called with the eggs and when she couldn't make Granny hear, had left them on the step.

She was full of tales and wisdom, and I recall her saying that after World War 1, she would often have six or seven tramps knock at the door. They did not ask for food, only for some water to fill their billy cans so that they could make a cup of tea. After receiving the hot water, they went on their way to the next workhouse. These were all men who had served their country in the War, but when peace came, they could find no work and took to the road.

Gran was a good friend to all who knew her and often left herself short in order to help others. When she died in 1962, she had just the change of £1 in her purse, but what a rich legacy she left us in her example of how to live a life with very little and be happy.

My great-granddad, Archelaus Whittle, was born in Winfrith in1861 and although I didn't know him personally, my father has told me numerous stories about him and what a character he was. His father died when he was young, leaving him and his siblings to do what they could to help their mother. Archelaus and his brother learnt how to live off their wits from an early age. It really was survival of the fittest. By nature, Archelaus was shrewd, kind, and witty. When he was married in 1886 to Jane Howard from Osmington, the couple moved to East Knighton, where they lived on the common in Poverty Row (since demolished), and this is where their eldest children were born.

Archelaus became a gamekeeper and as such would go on the local shoots. Once when eating his meal with the gentry and beaters, he was in conversation with one of the landowners who said, 'I like my potatoes floury, Whittle. How do you like yours?' Lifting his fork full of potatoes to his mouth, Archelaus replied, 'Up here on the fork!' He never worried about anything,

Archelaus Whittle in about the1930s

Mary Ann Bull, the reddlewoman

and when his wife or someone he knew was concerned how they were going to manage when another baby was on the way, he would say, 'Not to worry, just throw in another line of spuds.'

After moving to Belhuish, which is on the northern boundary of Lulworth, seven more children were born, giving them a family of seven sons and three daughters, my grandmother being one of the latter. The darts team at the local inn consisted of Archelaus and his boys, and they could often be seen walking across the fields on their way to the pub. He kept a donkey and cart, but their home was in a deep valley and whenever Archelaus went to catch the donkey, the creature would run away because he knew what was up ahead.

Local fairs were a chance for everyone to meet, and on 14 May the fair came to Wool (and still does). In Thomas Hardy's book, *The Return of the Native*, the reddleman plays a central part, and reddlemen were a common sight everywhere. Dorset was different as it had a reddlewoman, Mary Ann Bull, and every year on some common land near Archelaus's home, Mary Ann pitched her wagon. She had two fierce dogs and did not get on with people very well. Archelaus was the exception, and more than once he got into trouble with Jane when he came home with reddle on his clothes.

Archelaus made his own beer, and on one very rare occasion when a bout of influenza took him to his bed, the local doctor visited him. When the doctor caught sight of the bottles of beer, he told his patient, 'That beer will give you a slow death,' to which Archelaus replied, 'I'm in no hurry, doctor!'

Archelaus and Jane had a huge Bible and as each of their children was born, their name and date of birth were recorded on a page near the front of the Bible. He was a family man as well as a great character who took everything in his stride. During World War 1, when five of his sons were abroad fighting, some German prisoners of war were working on the farm and he would invite them in to his home to share a meal with him and Jane. It was a fitting testament to him as a great and compassionate humanitarian.

My paternal grandad, Henry Burt, known to all as Jack or Jacky, came from a long line of Dorset farm labourers. His father was the head carter on a rural Dorset estate and his mother was the local midwife, who could be seen walking the lanes and droves carrying a red spotted handkerchief and a pair of scissors as she made her way to a cottage where a mother was in labour.

Jack, who was born in 1886, acquired his nickname because as an adult he could run as fast as a jack hare and could catch them with his stick. He came from a large family where money was short, and his mother would make tea leaves by scraping the burnt pieces from a piece of toast. He left school at twelve years of age and as he was a short boy, found it hard to hold on to the two horses which pulled the plough.

Jack was a quiet man who led by example. As an adult and a married man, he had a strict routine each day. Every evening he would chop enough sticks to light the fire in the morning and then put them in the bread oven to dry out overnight. In the winter he would get up at 5 am to light the fire and put the kettle on to boil, which took one hour. While waiting for the kettle to boil, he would busy himself with other jobs, such as getting in enough logs for the day. He then had a cup of tea before going to work. In the summer he would get up earlier, as the working day started at 6 am. His whole life was very disciplined, which was not a problem for him. When breaking for lunch with the other farm workers, he would stand (never sit) at the end of the group, not wanting to be involved with any chit-chat, but preferring to have the company of another quiet soul. He never asked for anything and when he was asked, 'Are you happy, Jack?' he replied, 'I'm happy enough, thank you.'

Jack could turn his hand to most jobs on the farm and along with his brother, Fred, was a skilled hedger, which resulted in their photograph being printed in a national newspaper. He and his fellow farm labourers paid into a Slate Club every week, because if a farm worker became ill and could not work, his wages were stopped. Money from the Slate Club was given to the worker and his family to keep them from starvation. The farmer paid nothing.

He and his three brothers joined the army in World War 1, even though as farmworkers they were exempt. After returning safely home, they never spoke about their horrific ordeal, but could often be seen on their break quietly easing some shrapnel out of their skin. As Thomas Hardy said in his poem, 'Embarcation', when he saw the Dorsetshire Regiment off to war in 1899: 'None dubious of the cause, none murmuring.'

Jack lived until he was eighty-nine years old and when I think that he was born in William Barnes's lifetime, I remember Barnes's words when writing about the farmworkers: 'They talk of the unskilled labourer, I know of none.' We can learn much from these staunch, independent characters; as Virginia Woolf said about the ordinary characters in Hardy's novels, 'The peasants are the great sanctuary of sanity, the country the last stronghold of happiness. When they disappear, there is no hope for the race.'

Henry (Jack) Burt on the left, with two of his fellow farmworkers: in the middle Walter Downton and on the right Billy Bartlett

WHEN YOU GO HOME
TELL THEM OF US AND SAY
FOR YOUR TOMORROW
WE GAVE OUR TODAY

IN MEMORY
OF THE MEN
OF THE
2ND DIVISION
WHO FELL IN THE
BATTLE OF KOHIMA
AND
THE FIGHTING FOR
THE IMPHAL ROAD
APRIL 1944   JUNE 1944

In the footsteps of the brave

Peter Lush has made a pilgrimage to Kohima

Few of those attending Remembrance Services and Parades can be unaware of the words on the 2nd Division Memorial at Kohima: 'When you go home, tell them of us and say, for your tomorrow, we gave our today.' They are especially poignant to all true Dorset Men, as it was at Kohima that the 2nd Battalion of the Dorsetshire Regiment fought and triumphed in what was considered to be one of the most important battles of World War 2. According to the American historians, Alan Millet and Williamson Murray, who researched the battle, 'Nowhere in World War 2 – even on the Eastern Front – did the combatants fight with more mindless savagery.'

For a Dorset man, amateur military historian and father of a son who enlisted in the Devon and Dorsets (and is now a Major in The Rifles), the opportunity of a visit to the battlefield was irresistible, made more so as the specialist guide, Robert Lyman, was a good friend of mine who has written extensively on the Burma campaign, including Kohima 1944, and whom I had helped with his book, *Into the Jaws of Death*, about the raid on St Nazaire.

Kohima lies in Nagaland to the north-east of India, a few kilometres from the border with Burma. When, in 1944, the Japanese brought war to the Naga Hills, the Naga people fought with great determination and at no little cost. The help of these tenacious little warriors was of great benefit to the British and Indian troops who found themselves fighting in unfamiliar conditions in which the natives' knowledge was indispensable. A huge catalyst in this co-operation was the District Commissioner, Charles Pawsey MC, who cultivated them and for whom they would do anything. Charles Pawsey lived in the District Commissioner's bungalow on the lower terraces of the Kohima Ridge.

What follows is not a definitive history of the Kohima campaign but a description of the journey made by the 2nd Dorsets from Dimapur to Kohima in 1944 and the action in which they were involved when they got there, interspersed with my own progress along this route and over this battlefield in 2023. It was an experience to warm the heart and to stir the blood.

The 2nd Division memorial at Kohima

Charles Pawsey and 'his' Nagas with Lord Mountbatten

10 April 1944

March 1944 saw the 2nd Dorsets stationed in Ahmednagar, in western India, about to go on leave. However, the incursion of the Japanese army into India following their victory in Burma was to alter their plans dramatically. On the 28th they set off across the sub-continent and on 10 April, after a brief diversion to Bokajan in Assam, moved to Dimapur. This was an important centre for the British in their campaign against the Japanese as it boasted road and rail facilities through which to supply the British forces struggling to contain the Japanese push into India. It also had an airport which supplied the allied forces in Burma.

On 11 April, the 2nd Dorsets set off down the Manipur road to the relief of Kohima, 46 miles to the east. Crossing the Bailey bridge built across the Dhansiri river at Nichuguard, they progressed to milestone 31, where they were within sight of the enemy and where they took up a battalion position for the night, with B and D Companies being sent to nearby villages – B to Kiruphema, where they had their first spat with the enemy and suffered their first casualty, and D to Khabvuma. The next day, the rest of the battalion went forward to Zubza, where Bunker Hill had recently been cleared of the enemy by the Camerons, following an unsuccessful attempt by the Worcesters. The 7th Worcesters, the 1st Queens Own Cameron Highlanders and the 5th Field Ambulance RAMC, together with the 2nd Dorsets, made up 5th Brigade, 2nd Division.

On the following day, 12 April, the battalion, minus B and D Companies, moved into the perimeter at Zubza. Here the 5th Brigade, 2nd Division made its base and administrative area for the whole of the battle for Kohima.

On 13 April, D Company in the village of Khabvuma were set upon in no uncertain fashion by the enemy, who after a fierce battle withdrew. The burden of the attack fell upon 17 Platoon and resulted in the loss of four men.

During their progress from Dimapur to Kohima, the 2nd Dorsets rarely operated as a complete unit and were often hopelessly mixed up with units from other brigades. So it was that on 18 April, A and D Companies were sent to the Jotsoma area to operate with units of 6th Brigade. It was here at Jotsoma that Major-General J M L Grover set up his headquarters of 2nd Division, remembered today by an imposing notice on the roadside.

The Dorsets were split once again on 22 April, B and D Companies being taken by the battalion's second in command, Lt-Col 'Knocker' White, to relieve two companies of the Durhams on Piquet Hill, an isolated knoll to the west of Kohima which neatly covered the approach from Dimapur. From here they had a ringside seat to observe the fighting on the Kohima Ridge itself, a mere half-mile away. The objective was in sight, but it would be another few days before they would find themselves in the thick of the action.

26 January 2023

Our party, fourteen in number, gathered at Heathrow in the early hours of the morning for the flight to Calcutta. Getting to bed at half past midnight, we had to be up and away again at 3 am for our flight to Dimapur. Such a short stay was welcome, for the hotel was of a somewhat dubious standard and could well have been called 'The Black Hole'.

First impressions of Dimapur were that, although jungle was the predominant feature of the landscape, we were never out of sight of a dwelling, for they lined the road at regular intervals: my pre-tour vision of Kohima being 'in the jungle' was to be shattered. Our first stop, after ten miles, was at Nichuguard to visit the Bailey bridge, which still exists although now by-passed by a more modern crossing. If men and

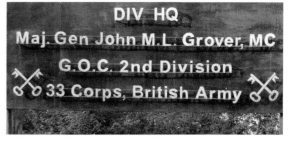

The sign to Major-General Grover's divisional headquarters remains by the roadside at Jotsoma

The Bailey bridge at Nichuguard:
If it didn't fly to Imphal, it crossed this bridge.

materiel did not fly to Imphal, they went over this bridge. Robert Lyman left us in no doubt of the importance of this crossing and we marvelled that such a relatively small structure could carry so much.

Continuing our journey down the Manipur Road, we next stopped at Zubza, where the Japanese had established the road-block which was cleared by the Cameron Highlanders. From our vantage point on Zubza Plateau, looking down on Zubza itself, we caught our first glimpse of the Kohima Ridge, away in the hazy distance. This was clearly an important vantage point and it was easy to understand the difficulty of dislodging the enemy.

As we continued to Kohima, we were looking forward to reaching our hotel, a good meal and a comfortable bed after a long day's travel. Tired though we may have been, it had taken the Dorsets fifteen days to reach the ridge and their trial of strength with the Japanese was yet to reach its climax.

Kohima Ridge

Kohima is the capital of Nagaland and now boasts a population of 100,000. The verdant jungle that I had expected was nowhere in evidence. Jungle there is, but it is now one of concrete. The Kohima Ridge itself sits in the middle of this sprawling metropolis and is a dominant feature. The ridge runs roughly due west and comprises four terraces, separated by steep drops varying between ten and forty feet. Above them is the solid mass of Garrison Hill.

Topmost of the terraces in 1944 was the club square, where badminton was played, dropping to the tennis court, destined to enter the annals of history for ever. Then came the largest drop to the District Commissioner's bungalow, and the last level was the lower garden where now stands the Kohima Memorial. On the south face of the ridge ran the drive to the District Commissioner's bungalow, passing the residence of the Commandant of the Assam Rifles.

26 April 1944

B and D Companies of the 2nd Dorsets entered Garrison Hill, above the ridge, by way of a slope criss-crossed by sniper fire and lost sixteen men in doing so. Battalion HQ was also established on the hill. They had entered a battlefield so small and so encumbered with men that it was confusing in the extreme, made worse by the fact that it was impossible to see one level of the ridge from another.

That night, A and C Companies were ordered to attack, with C joining the Royal Berkshire Regiment in a foray against the enemy on the corner of the tennis court. They took out a large bunker on the north-east corner, while A traversed the northern slope of the ridge below the tennis court to occupy the District Commissioner's bungalow. Early success could not be maintained and they were driven to the point of the ridge below the lower garden. They were told to hold it at all costs. They did. Such night actions do not come without a cost and the battalion lost 28 men on 27 April. That day Battalion HQ on Garrison Hill was also shelled.

On the 28th, an attempt was made to get a tank onto the tennis court, but it failed, as did a further attempt on the 30th, when the Stuart tank involved first broke down and then ran out of petrol. On 2 May, A Company found themselves under fire from a Japanese 75mm gun and the next day were relieved by B Company, who were welcomed by a fierce onslaught. A Company had held out for five and a half days and, totally exhausted, were sent in reserve to Dimapur.

The District Commissioner's bungalow before and after the battle

Yet another effort to get a tank onto the tennis court took place on the 4th by the simple expedient of taking it up the drive to the District Commissioner's bungalow. It was joined by B Company, but they were driven back. The next day they tried again, this time with a little more success, and got into the bungalow, but the tank could not climb the steep bank to the tennis court and once again they had to retire. Although the Japanese commander had made the tennis court a strongpoint and it had become a death trap, they now felt they were getting the measure of the enemy. Two days of attrition followed, but B Company still held the lower garden.

There was now an intense battle across the whole of the Kohima Ridge and losses mounted, but the situation was much improved by the arrival on Garrison Hill of the Rajputs, who did not share the British reluctance to clear the jungle and set to work cutting down trees. This opened up the Japanese positions on about three-quarters of the tennis court and also the bungalow, making them visible from the club terrace.

On 11 May C Company carried out a pincer attack from the south flank and the next day the Royal Engineers bulldozed a track up which a tank was dragged. The battle was edging away from the Japanese and the next day, together with elements of B and D Companies, a tank finally made it on to the tennis court, paving the way for final success. The Kohima Ridge had been cleared of the enemy.

27 January 2023

What was to be a momentous day dawned bright and clear. We entered the ridge along the driveway to the District Commissioner's bungalow and made our way directly to the lowest point of the battlefield, the lower garden, where men of the 2nd Dorsets had held their ground throughout the action by the battalion. Here stood the Kohima Memorial, with those iconic words which I had heard at so many Remembrance Services. The hairs on the back of my neck were doing overtime, and yet it was somehow unreal in another sense. You only had to turn through 180 degrees to come face to face with the new jungle of concrete blocks and bamboo scaffolding lining the road from Dimapur to Imphal where it swung right round the point of the Ridge.

After a full explanation of the battle from Robert Lyman, we set off

The arrival of this tank on the debris-strewn tennis court turned the course of the battle

up the various terraces to Garrison Hill at the top. The entire ridge is now the Commonwealth War Graves Commission cemetery, where the dead from the action lie virtually where they fell. It is unique in being the only cemetery that the CWGC has built on the actual battlefield. In doing so, the Commission has performed a unique service to the remembrance of this crucial action, for by using the ground thus, it has forestalled the inevitable outcome that the ridge itself would have joined the concrete jungle. I thank them for it with all my heart.

The terraces swept ever upward and even with modern steps, it was no easy climb. The first terrace is now a car park, an essential facility for those visiting the site, but there is no trace of the District Commissioner's bungalow that once stood there. This leads to a further level where are many of the graves of the fallen including, on the northern side, the Dorset plot. Here, among others, lies Arthur David Deane, with whose brother I played golf at Came Down, where a seat is placed in his memory. I was pleased to be able to pay my respects.

The next climb, perhaps the steepest and certainly the longest, brought us to the tennis court. Here is the Cross of Sacrifice, a feature of all CWGC cemeteries, erected on the edge of the court, which is now permanently marked out in white stone. This must be one of the most iconic sites in all of Dorset's proud and extensive military history and I certainly wrestled with my own emotions. Local youngsters wandered respectfully across it and it was good to see that their generation has not forgotten the heroism of years ago that liberated their town.

A further sharp set of steps brought me to the club square, again with the graves laid out in the neat, well-kept rows that typify such cemeteries, and finally to the Stone of Remembrance, another constant feature of CWGC sites. Here the cemetery ended but behind the Stone, inaccessible to us, rose the final feature of the Ridge, Garrison Hill. Almost incongruously, it now bears many trees and is dotted with houses.

I could not resist a last visit to the Kohima Memorial at the very foot of the ridge. I would not come this way again and I wanted this to be my last memory. Remembrance Sunday will have added significance this year and the Kohima Epitaph will bring back amazing memories. Rest easy, heroes. I am going home, and I will tell them of you.

The tennis court today

The Sentinel

There, seen upon far distant hill, this finger held on high
Cries out to all who pass this way and question as to why
It found its place, or yet the mark it makes to such as me,
To sentinel these fielded lands and know its destiny.

This tower stands of brick and stone to face cold winter's blast,
This monument to man or deeds from long-forgotten past.
What tale of fortitude or chance might it to us relate?
What caused which others to want it there to register – whose fate?

And so the reason is enquired, an explanation sought,
Since surely some must know the word of why it all was wrought,
But answers leave confusion sown while many others said
That this was just a folly built by idle wealth, now dead.

Yet now we have a truth, it seems, for now a name is known:
It stands above in memory of one whose time has flown,
A man to laud the lands about this Dorset through his pen,
For this is Hardy's tower, was for Thomas builded then.

Upon this information I then quickened to that hill,
Through lanes and past the places which he may have travelled – still
He sits in pensive statue set in Dorchester nearby –
I come at last upon the sight against an azure sky.

Laid out below extends the green to vistas of blue seas
And off to Portland Bill beyond and Weymouth. Such as these
Remain the beating heart he knew and much he wrote in praise,
And so I near the plaques that speak of this famed writer's days.

But no! This is the given name, but not the same I thought;
Though it is Thomas Hardy here, 'tis one whose battles fought
Included famed Trafalgar and through Nelson is he known,
The story of that Victory recorded in this stone.

Erected by his shipmates as the officers and men
Remembered 'Kiss me Hardy', which a dying Nelson then
Was said to speak those final words to this his trusted friend,
And him on whom I now reflect as downward roads I wend.

Yes, should you ever journey to this place of ancient lore,
From Arthur onto Romans here they left their sign and more,
You should take time in due respect, once noted far away,
The lofty Hardy's Tower standing proud until this day.

John Seymour

Hubs, spokes and felloes

Russell Randall has been a wheelwright for almost 40 years. He and his son are the only true wheelwrights still working in Dorset. John Newth has been to meet him.

The website of the Worshipful Company of Wheelwrights sets out to list all those still working at the craft in the UK. It is not a long list, with barely 40 names on it, and only one of those is in Dorset: Russell Randall of Litton Cheney. Russell is a general carpenter and joiner as well as a wheelwright, but his skill at the centuries-old craft is in keeping with his attitude to his work generally: 'I'm very traditional and still do things using old-fashioned methods. Why? Because they were developed over the years by

Russell Randall in the doorway of his Litton Cheney workshop

generations of skilled craftsmen, and they work. Not only that, they produce things that last longer than machine-made modern pieces. Of course we use drills but mostly I still prefer a hand tool to a battery drill.' Russell still works in imperial measurements because 'I've found it good enough for the last 67 years,

The wooden constituents of a basic wheel: the hub, a spoke and a felloe

so why change?' Challenged that it is harder to calculate in feet and inches than in metric, he responds, 'As long as you know your times tables, you're all right.'

Generations of Randalls have worked with wood: as carpenters and before that as sawyers back to 1700. Russell is actually following in his uncle's footsteps rather than those of his father, who moved to Dorset from the family's traditional base in Beckington, Somerset, to Dorset and spent his working life in agriculture, mostly as a shepherd. Russell served his apprenticeship with C E Slade & Sons of Dorchester, a general building firm whose works were in Acland Road, and continued to work for them until they were taken over. He was then a foreman joiner with C G Fry, whose base is in Litton Cheney, for eight years before setting up his own business in 1986.

Russell has been joined in the business by his son, Chris, and together they do a lot of work on listed buildings, making staircases, doors and windows. They create some furniture, and the variety of jobs is something Russell enjoys: 'When you've worked on a complicated Georgian staircase for six to eight weeks, it's nice to come back to something rather more simple.'

Russell learnt how to make wheels by watching others and teaching himself. Chris did what was then the only available course in the subject, at Hereford College. He won the award for top student, but the course no longer exists, although there is an apprenticeship scheme supported by the Worshipful Company. Although the market has inevitably declined, Russell still finds customers among those who collect old vehicles – he and Chris are about to start on the complete restoration of an old Dorset waggon for one such collector – and those who drive them for sport or as a hobby. The biggest wheel

Russell ever made was a 5' 6" monster for the first replica of George III's bathing machine that the local council installed near the King's Statue in Weymouth some 30 years ago.

Making a wheel starts with using a lathe to turn the hub, which is made of elm because it is a tough, fibrous wood resistant to splitting under the enormous forces to which the hub is subject. However, it is fitted with two metal bands, one inside, one outside, to reinforce the wood's natural strength. Tapered holes are cut in the hub for the spokes, which are made of oak because of its longitudinal strength; as the wheel turns, each spoke is momentarily doing all the load-bearing work of that wheel.

The outer wooden circle of the wheel is made up of curved sections called felloes (pronounced 'fellies'), usually one for every two spokes. These are mostly made from ash, which has a natural springiness, and great skill is called for in calculating and cutting exactly the right degree of curve. Finally, the metal rim is added. This is called the bond, which is appropriate as it pulls everything together. A circle of metal, carefully measured to the right length, is heated on a simple bonfire so that it expands and can be slipped over the wooden circle of felloes. Cold water is then thrown over it and it quickly contracts back to its

Chris Randall admires the framework for the entrance to a Dorset barn conversion on which he and his father are working

original diameter and not only fits snugly over the wheel but also compresses it so that all the joints are solid and tight.

The result is not only a new, perfectly made and fully functional wheel but also a thing of beauty. As George Sturt wrote in his book, *The Wheelwright's Shop*, every curve of a finished wheel tells of the skill that has been bestowed upon it – the skill of a man like Russell Randall.

Russell Randall built this hearse some years ago for a Weymouth funeral director

David Downton and friends. In front: David, Roy Fursey, Tom Gill. Behind: John Howard.

The Victoria Park Olympics

David Downton tells how the youth of Dorchester celebrated the legendary 1948 Games

I was eleven in 1948, attending Dorchester Grammar School with many friends from around Dagmar and Olga Roads in Victoria Park, Dorchester, who are sadly almost all deceased. The 1948 post-war Olympic Games were staged in London, the first Summer Olympics held since the 1936 Games in Berlin. Times were still austere in Britain and would continue to be so for some time. Here was no Olympic Village: male competitors were accommodated in military camps in Uxbridge and West Drayton, while the ladies were housed in several London colleges.

Athletes provided their own kit and because there was still rationing, competitors were allowed the same rations as workers in 'heavy industries' like miners and dockers, who received 5467 calories instead of the normal 2600. Some countries also brought additional food – foremost of course were the Americans, who could not do without steak! This was the last Games to include arts in the schedule, which took place in the Victoria and Albert Museum. Medals were awarded for painting, music, sculpture, literature and architecture on themes related to sport.

My friends warmed to the idea of staging our own Olympic Games around the alley backs and roads where we lived. Hardly anyone owned a car, so we were always able to play in streets usually devoid of traffic. It is fair to say that we 'owned the streets'!

In order to fund refreshments, which were only consumed at the end of events, I made a puppet theatre from scrap wood and scrounged old clothes, then prior to the Games, with puppets borrowed from friends, gave puppet shows with a small entrance fee. I bought bottles of Corona lemonade and freshly baked bread from the cake shop at the end of Cambridge Road. Parents were alerted that we would not be in for meals that Saturday because we were playing 'Olympics', and this was accepted because we normally played outside and had to be called in for meals.

The Dorchester Olympics lacked not only nude discus-throwers but the razzmatazz that accompanied even the 'austerity' Olympics

Our Games were also very austere, but we made a profit. It was agreed to charge each competitor a halfpenny and award a prize of twopence to the winner of each event. We failed to take on board that awarding cash prizes was against the amateur sprit of this sporting event and made us professionals! However, with hindsight I think the entries would have been fewer without the cash incentive for some competitors. Twopence went a long way in the 'forties!

Our track events included sprints around the alley backs dividing Dagmar and Olga Roads: once, five and ten times around. The marathon would

be won by whoever could outrun everyone until they were the last boy running.
I can remember winning that event and slept very soundly that evening! The
Games went on until it was dark and our mothers had to come and fetch us in,
exhausted.

Some of my friends taking part were John Howard, Royston Fursey,
Bryan Furmage, Tommy Gill, Graham Osborne, Peter Clark, Geoffrey Budd,
Dennis Babb, Michael Clark and my brother, Adrian Downton. The Victoria Park
Olympic Games also included go-cart and bicycle races, which caused many cuts
and grazes because of the uneven surface of the alley backs. Because we were a
competitive lot, several competitors were thrown from their go-carts or bikes
into nettles in the alley and their wounds were either bound with handkerchiefs
or soothed with dock leaves. Events in Olga Road were limited to putting the
shot (which was half a brick), archery and freewheeling go-cart races.

Elderly residents enjoyed watching us compete and brought out their
cups of tea and cakes. None had their eyes knocked out by stray arrows, but
there were one or two near misses. Anyhow, people knew how to duck and run,
having been ducking and diving for six years of war. Road-sweepers stopped to
enjoy the spectacle of children heaving half-bricks in the air onto the council's
roads and not a single injunction followed our pitting of the road surface.

We had a proper awards ceremony where victors received their cash prize
standing on a soapbox. But that was not all they received. I decided that winners
of the most prestigious events should receive a proper medal and my only source
was the medals my father had received for his service in World War 2, which
included the Italian Star and the Africa Star. I obviously had no idea what these
meant to him, but the following November, come Remembrance Day, I heard
a frustrated and later exasperated Dad searching for his medals to wear at the
service at Dorchester's Cenotaph, which was an important event for him and
his friends who had served their country. I slunk out to my friends' houses with
fingers crossed and fortunately they all still had the medals and I was able to
sheepishly return them to my father. I think he secretly saw the funny side of it,
but he never let on and was pretty angry.

My punishment was to lose my sweet ration for a month. Sweets were
still on ration, as were many other things after the war. This was harsh, but not as
big a deal as I made it out to be. Those of us who had cycled, go-carted, heaved
half-bricks and fired bows and arrows together stuck together, so I was never
short of sweets during the embargo!

Whichever way the winds blow we will ensure you arrive in the right place.

#established1858

Symonds&Sampson

Churchill's secret army in Dorset

Andy Sturgess pays tribute to the almost unimaginable bravery of the 'stay behind' units

May 1940. France has fallen and the invasion of Britaion is regarded as a certainty. Ideas for defiant defence are being hatched everywhere, not least in the fertile mind of Winston Churchill, who has been prime minister for less than a month. One of his ideas is for a 'stay behind' army of guerrilla units, whose role will be to go into hiding as the Germans advance and then operate behind the lines to cause as much damage as possible to the enemy's arteries of communication and supply.

In utmost secrecy, small but well-trained groups, known as Auxiliary Units, were established. In the event of an invasion they were to go to ground in secret underground bunkers and stay put for about two weeks, then emerge and quietly disrupt the enemy in any way they could. The ideal recruits, who were mostly found in the fledgling Home Guard, were men in reserved occupations who knew their local area intimately and were physically fit. It followed that a high proportion of them were farmworkers, foresters, gamekeepers – and poachers.

Teams were built up in secret and were given uniforms like the Home

The entrance to the Beaminster bunker

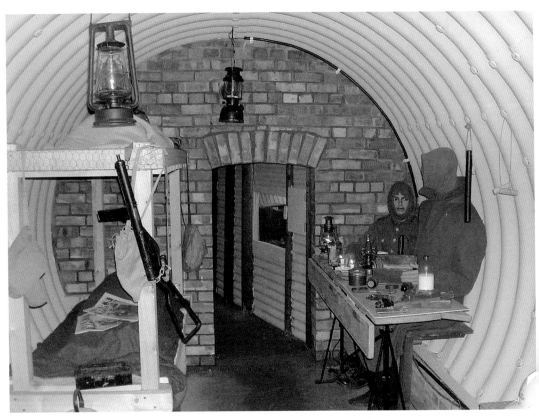

Above: This reconstruction of a typical operating base is at the
British Resistance Organisation Museum at Parham, Suffolk

Below:The emergency exit from the Beaminster OB

Guard so as not to stand out, the only difference being the badge they wore. Recruits were sent by train to a village called Highworth in Wiltshire, where they had to report to two old ladies in the local Post Office. From there they were transported by covered lorry to Coles Hill House, where they spent two weeks learning all the skills they needed for their intended role: unarmed combat, use of firearms, explosives and the other requirements of guerilla warfare. They discovered that stretching a piano wire across a road to bring off an enemy dispatch rider was easy; the clever part was angling the wire so that the body ended up in the ditch, where it could be more easily disposed of. Their operating manual was disguised as a catalogue for 'Highworth Fertiliser' and hung in many farmhouse kitchens in plain sight. In Dorset, training was also carried out at Duntish Court, a now-demolished country house at Buckland Newton.

Even as early as May 1940, the Nazis' willingness to use civilians to their evil ends was well known. The activities of the Auxiliary Units would surely have led to reprisals against the civilian population and this consequence was discussed at as high a level as the War Cabinet. What was even more obvious was that serving in an Auxiliary Unit that had been overrun by the Germans' advance could only be a suicide mission. The greater the success a unit enjoyed, the greater would be the enemy's efforts to destroy it: its extinction could only be a matter of time. The ordinary Englishmen (and a few Englishwomen) who joined the units were surely aware of this, and their courage is something at which later generations can only wonder and be humble.

There were several units in Dorset, but here I'll mention just two of them. One was based in a bunker in a small wood up on

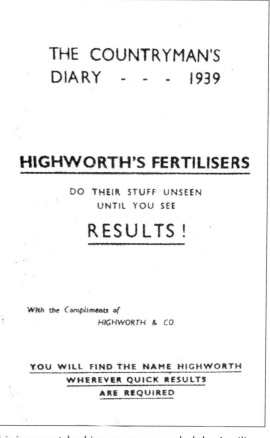

THE COUNTRYMAN'S
DIARY - - - 1939

HIGHWORTH'S FERTILISERS

DO THEIR STUFF UNSEEN
UNTIL YOU SEE

RESULTS !

With the Compliments of
HIGHWORTH & CO.

YOU WILL FIND THE NAME HIGHWORTH
WHEREVER QUICK RESULTS
ARE REQUIRED

This innocent-looking cover concealed the Auxiliary Units' operating manual the downs above Beaminster. It was known as an 'OB', or operating base, and, equipped with food, arms and explosives, could accommodate about twelve people. It was built in total secrecy right under the nose of the farmer who owned the land, who never knew that it was there or that his son was actually trained and part of the group. A searchlight or anti-aircraft gun was located on the site and guarded, keeping onlookers away while the Royal Engineers built the bunker. They had a lot of excavated chalk to dispose of. Solution: put it in piles across the downs at night and with explosives blow it sky-high to make it look as if a string of bombs had been dropped! No one would question the resulting holes in a neat line the next day.

If the Beaminster OB was typical (and the bunkers did vary slightly), it consisted of an underground construction of concrete blocks or bricks with a corrugated iron roof. It would have been divided into two, with a living area that also served as storage for the deadly tools of the resistance fighter's trade, and a sleeping area with hammocks arranged in the shape of a star, the foot ends being tied to a pole in the centre.

The father of a friend of mine told us about the Beaminster bunker back in the 1960s, but it was not easy to find as it had a concealed entrance and was well camouflaged. It survived the war and was only recently destroyed by the current landowner. Fortunately, I managed to revisit some years ago and take some photographs to make sure its memory was secured.

At the other end of the county, in Norden Wood on the north side of Knowle Hill, was the bunker that was home to one of the Auxiliary Units on the Isle of Purbeck. Its leader was Sergeant Fred Simpson, who was employed as a farmworker by Jack Baggs of Wareham. After the war he farmed on his own account at Claypole and Goathorn Farms, near the Purbeck shore of Poole Harbour. His second-in-command, Doug Green, was also a farmworker, while other members of the group worked in the clay mines of Purbeck.

Fred and Doug once received a crate of a dozen phosphorus grenades with orders to store them under water. The ground around their base had a high water-table, so it was no trouble to dig a hole to hide the crate. Unfortunately, they forgot to mark the spot and although they tried many times after the war, they never managed to locate the grenades – so somewhere under that patch of Purbeck heath lurks a lethal reminder of those desperate days. Another reminder came when someone showed Fred Simpson some capsules they had found. He immediately recognised them as the cyanide pills that were issued to all members of the Auxiliary Units so that they should not reveal under interrogation the location of their base.

Later in the war, it was realised that invasion was not a problem, but rather than waste the highly trained personnel of the Auxiliary Units, some became part of secret operations and were parachuted into Europe as part of SOE, or joined what we now know as the SAS. Others left for Europe on D-Day via Tarrant Rushton airfield. Having signed the Official Secrets Act, many of the men of the Auxiliary Units never talked about it until over 50 years after the war's end, if at all. Some had been labelled as draft-dodgers locally because they were still working in the countryside as others went to war; ironically, most of these men had been better trained than others in the forces at that time, but could not tell anyone what they did. It all goes to show how reliable and resourceful Dorset countrymen can be when called upon by their country in time of need.

www.parhamairfieldmuseum.co.uk/british-resistance-organisation/

Above: Sergeant Fred Simpson

Below: The Norden Wood unit, christened the 'Creech Barrow Seven' although its OB was some way from Creech Barrow, is remembered by a memorial in Purbeck stone by the entrance to Kilwood Nature Reserve, near East Creech

THE
CREECH BARROW
SEVEN
AUXILIARY UNIT
G.H.Q. HOME FORCES

1940 - 1944

Sgt. FRED SIMPSON
Cpl. DOUG GREEN
Pte. LES GREEN
Pte. HAROLD HATCHARD
Pte. JACK HATCHARD
Pte. ELI KITCATT
Pte. WILF STOCKLEY

MAY THEY REST IN PEACE
IN THE LAND THEY WERE
PREPARED TO DEFEND
WHEN IT WAS IN
MORTAL DANGER

Forde Abbey

Tucked away in the far west of the county is arguably its finest historic house. Andrew Headley celebrates its physical beauty and its historical and architectural interest.

What do you do when you find yourself with a redundant 55Kw pump that was once used for the irrigation of soft fruit on your estate? Obviously, you use it to create a *jet d'eau* which sends a single plume of white water 160 feet (nearly 50 metres) into the air, the highest powered fountain in the country. That is what the Roper family did in 2005 to mark the centenary of their coming to Forde Abbey. It was a rare flash of flamboyance for the Ropers, whose attitude has always been to let the historical and architectural interest of the house and the beauty of the gardens speak for themselves. No roundabouts on the lawn or lions in the park for them: 'I couldn't think of anything worse,' says Alice Kennard (née Roper), who with her husband, Julian, is the current occupant and custodian of the house.

They took over in 2009 when Mark Roper, Alice's father, felt that he should stand back from the management of the estate, which is close to the point where Dorset, Somerset and Devon meet. He also wanted Alice's children to grow up in the house, the responsibility for which would one day pass to them. He continued to take a close interest until his death two years ago, and staff became used to making sure that everything was on the top line before Mark arrived in his buggy for a noon inspection. He had earned the right because he had looked after the estate for 33 years and had won great respect for a forward-looking programme of improvements which did not interfere with the unique qualities of the house and gardens; he liked to quote from *The Leopard* by Giuseppe Tomasi di Lampedusa: 'If we want things to go on as they are, we have to change.' Many of the improvements were carried out with the help of Richard Tyler, a distinguished architect who had worked on Salisbury Cathedral and Knebworth House among other historic buildings. It was Richard Tyler who shrewdly observed, 'The great thing about Forde Abbey is that for the past 300 years, none of its owners has been rich enough to seriously mess it up.'

Abbot Chard's porch

Mark had inherited from his father, Geoffrey, who in all lived at Forde for almost eighty years, being the son of the first Roper to live there: Elizabeth, who was born Elizabeth Evans. Before the Evanses, the property belonged briefly to a Mr Miles from Bristol, who bought it in 1846 when the then owner, John Gwyn, died childless. The Gwyns had married into the Prideaux family, so there was an unbroken line of succession of almost two centuries back to Edmund Prideaux, MP for Lyme Regis, who took over a rather dilapidated Forde Abbey in 1649.

Edmund made major improvements, including the creation of the Saloon and the Grand Staircase. There is a theory that Inigo Jones worked on the house, but that is unlikely since Jones was a fervent Royalist, while Edmund was committed to the Parliamentarian cause, ending up as Attorney General to Oliver Cromwell. His son, also Edmund, took a financial blow as a result of entertaining the Duke of Monmouth to dinner once, in 1680. Five years later, after Monmouth's abortive attempt to oust his uncle, James II, Judge Jeffries took that dinner to mean that Prideaux must have been a supporter of the rebellion and had him locked up in the Tower of London. It cost Prideaux £15,000 (equivalent to £2½ million today) to escape the gallows.

The Saloon

The Bentham Room

For more than a century before the arrival of the Prideauxs, Forde Abbey had mouldered away under various absentee owners following the Dissolution of the Monasteries in 1539. As a Cistercian monastery for four hundred years, it had become one of the wealthiest religious houses in the country, so was a prime target for Henry VIII's grab. The last in its long line of Abbots was Thomas Chard, who remodelled the house between 1521 and 1539, including the creation of the Great Hall and the porch with its magnificent two-storey oriel window. He allowed himself some evidence of his pride in his work: on the parapet of the porch is a Latin inscription that translates as 'Made by Abbot Thomas Chard, master, AD 1528'. Some historians claim that Chard was far-sighted enough to see what was coming and purposely invested the monastery's wealth in its buildings, but there is no evidence to support this.

The porch leads into the Great Hall, noted for its wonderful painted ceiling. It was even larger, but Edmund Prideaux shortened it as part of his overall plan for the Abbey. The Abbey church itself was destroyed at the time of the Dissolution, but two relics of it are to be seen here: a statue of St Catherine, who has lost her head but can be identified by the wheel she is holding, and one of St Margaret, who was the daughter of an exiled Anglo-Saxon prince and ended up marrying the King of Scotland. The Great Hall occasionally hosts plays and concerts, for which it is an ideal venue.

Prideaux's Grand Staircase, notable for its intricately carved balustrade and its elaborate ceiling, leads up to the first floor, where the main room is the Saloon. This was described by a previous occupant of the house with pride and not without justification as 'the best room in Dorset'. The architectural historian, Nikolaus Pevsner, refers to the room's 'noble restraint'. The Prideaux coat of arms forms the centre of the impressive plaster ceiling and is surrounded by biblical scenes. On the walls hang the Mortlake Tapestries, woven from cartoons by Raphael which were created by him as originals for tapestries for the Sistine Chapel in the Vatican. Again the themes are Biblical, mostly showing scenes from the lives of St Peter and St Paul.

The Cloisters

The tapestries were commissioned by Edmund Prideaux but confiscated before they could be delivered because of his son's presumed support of the Duke of Monmouth. For thirty years they lay rolled up in Whitehall until Queen Anne presented them to Francis Gwyn as a mark of favour for his work as her Secretary of War. Queen Anne died before she could make a planned visit to Forde Abbey but the Gwyns had already had a fine four-poster bed made for her use. Today it is in the Bentham Room, named after the utilitarian philosopher who rented the Abbey from the Gwyns not long before it was sold out of the family, and whose bedroom it was.

Among other notable rooms on the first floor is the Upper Refectory, which houses an oak table 21 feet long and made in 1948 of three planks from a single tree on the estate. It is 2¼ feet wide, and there is a story that it was supposed to be 3¼ feet but the maker could not read Geoffrey Roper's handwriting! There are two refectories in the Abbey because in the 15th century, Cistercians were allowed to eat meat for the first time. Some of the monks vehemently opposed this change, so they continued to eat in the original refectory, while the carnivores migrated to the Upper Refectory.

Of interest to social historians is the replica of a servant's room of the early 18th century, which Alice Kennard created from one of the original monk's cells. The basic nature of the room and its sparse furnishings must have provided minimal comfort after its occupant's 15-hour working day.

Back on the ground floor, the Cloisters are all that remains of what would have been a rectangle, with the Abbey church forming one side. They were renovated by Thomas Chard and today are a light, atmospheric space, often filled with colourful plants. Just outside the house is the Chapel, created by Edmund Prideaux from the Chapter House, where the monks would have attended to the Abbey's substantial business interests. It is notable for its plain but pleasing 12th-century vaulting. The Chapel is still used for services and is open even when the house is closed.

The Abbey Yard

For many, the greatest glory of Forde Abbey is its gardens. They were largely created by Francis Gwyn and his wife, Margaret (née Prideaux), but successive Gwyns and Ropers have cherished and developed them – Geoffrey Roper, for example, planted 350,000 trees on the estate. In 1914 there were ten full-time gardeners but today there is only one full-timer and two part-timers, although Alice Kennard takes an enthusiastic interest and qualifies as a third part-timer. She herself created the Winter Garden, whose name is self-explanatory, and the Spiral Garden, inspired by the penitential spiral used by monks for meditation; it is planted with 6000 tulips.

The gardens cover 30 acres in all, a mixture of individual gardens, open spaces and an extensive arboretum. Statues are dotted through the gardens, including a copy of the rearing stallion that stands outside the National Stud at Newmarket, and a charmingly appropriate figure of Alice in Wonderland in the Kitchen Garden.

A short description of Forde Abbey can only cherry-pick its outstanding features. One of the pleasures of the place, particularly its gardens, is that you never know what you are going to stumble on round the next corner. It is possible to be there for a whole day without discovering all its delights – but it will still have been a day well spent.

www.fordeabbey.co.uk

The Spiral Garden

Holes Bay provides a backdrop for an Upton House parkrun

Running free

Dorset has embraced the global parkrun phenomenon and brings to the party some spectacular locations, as Richard Pilcher describes

'…the here and now: grab at happiness as it flies by.' J.L. Carr: A Month in the Country

October 2024 will mark the twentieth anniversary of the inaugural parkrun event, which was held in Bushy Park, London, with just thirteen runners. There are now over five million participants worldwide running at over 1700 events in more than 23 countries. They are free, fun and inclusive events, which happen every Saturday at 9 am. The 5-km course is undertaken by all ages and includes runners, wheelchair users, joggers and walkers, not to mention dogs on leads and a few babies in prams. Participants range 'from elite athletes to those who just want to keep going!'

Registering online before your first parkrun is essential. Google 'parkrun' and follow the instructions at www.parkrun.org.uk. You only need to do it once. Print out your personalised barcode, which enables you to have your attendance and time recorded at the end of the run: 'no barcode, no time'. Your barcode is valid for always at all parkruns throughout the world. All details about the nearest course and its location are also available on the parkrun website.

Volunteers organise all aspects of the event and without them there would be no parkruns. There are about 40 volunteers for each event. Offering to volunteer is via the email address for that particular parkrun. Helping with and taking part in these local community events has been shown to be of tremendous benefit for both mental and physical health. Volunteering jobs are varied and provide opportunities to put personal skills to good use. Without doubt, the most valuable of these is the ability to give a warm welcome and provide a friendly face. Apart from organisers such as the race director and marshals, other roles include helping to set up and take down the course, to tail runners and to write it all up.

Support is also provided by official companies whose merchandise includes milestone T-shirts, snoods, hoodies, personalised water bottles, pin badges and barcoded wrist bands. Profits from the purchase of merchandise from these official sponsors help to fund parkruns and keep them free. 2023 saw the launching of an official parkrun magazine.

About fifteen minutes before the run starts, a first timers' briefing is given to those new to parkruns in general or to that particular course. Words of welcome are also given by the race director, which include updates on the condition of the course and the presence of any potential hazards. Reminders include 'It's a run not a race' and to always give priority to others who are not parkrunners but are sharing the same public space.

Post-parkrun coffee is at a designated café close to the finishing area. Here the feelgood factor of having taken part and the palpable upbeat mood for the start of the weekend may be shared with other members of the parkrun community.

Runners flanked by the Great Globe and the sea during a parkrun
at Durlston Country Park in June 2023

At the time of writing there are nine parkruns in Dorset:

- Blandford parkrun (Jubilee Way)
- Bournemouth parkrun (King's Park Athletic Stadium)
- Durlston Country Park parkrun (Swanage)
- Moors Valley parkrun (Country Park and Forest, nr Ringwood)
- Poole parkrun (Poole Park)
- St Mary's parkrun (St Mary's Park, Bridport)
- The Great Field parkrun (Poundbury, Dorchester)
- Upton House parkrun (Upton Country Park, Poole)
- Weymouth parkrun (Lodmoor Country Park)

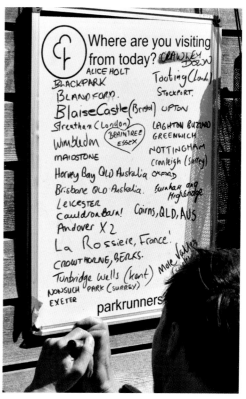

The visitors board at the Durlston Country Park parkrun. Runners from as close as Blandford Forum and as far afield as France and Australia record their attendance.

In addition, Dorset has four juniors parkruns which are held on Sunday mornings at 9 am. These are 2 km in length and are exclusively for 4- to 14-year-olds. They provide a great opportunity to get children into regular exercise. Current venues are:

- Bournemouth (Ensbury Avenue, Slades Park)
- The Great Field (Poundbury, Dorchester)
- Upton House (Upton Country Park, Poole)
- Weymouth (Lodmoor Country Park)

Numbers of Dorset parkruns are steadily increasing, so it is worth checking online for updates. Below are some details of those I can speak of personally. I look forward in time to participating in the rest.

Blandford comprises a straight run along the old North Dorset Trailway, part of the former rail line which fell victim to Dr Beeching in the 1960s and now serves as a long-distance trail for walkers, runners and cyclists.

Durlston Country Park parkrun at Swanage has been put forward as being 'the most beautiful and toughest in the parkrun world' (see YouTube under the title 'The most beautiful parkrun in the world / Durlston Country Park').

Coming uphill from 'Tilly Whim Caves corner' in Durlston Country Park. One runner described Durlston as the toughest course out of the 250 that they had undertaken!

The brutal route incorporates part of the South West Coast Path and boasts stunning views with Durlston Castle, Tilly Whim Caves and the Great Globe along the route. The last is constructed of Portland stone and is one of the largest stone spheres in the world. It weighs about 40 tons and is surrounded by stone plaques with quotations including some from English literature, Roman poets and the Bible. Durlston Castle café serves post-run coffee on its elevated terrace with panoramic views across Swanage Bay to the Isle of Wight and the Dorset coastline.

Poole parkrun attracts the largest average number of runners in Dorset with about 600 taking part each week. It starts near the cricket pavilion in Poole Park and is run on tarmac and compacted gravel with two laps around the pond there. On 24 December 2022, a new women's parkrun world record was set here by Welsh athlete Melissa Courtney-Bryant with a time of 15 minutes and 31 seconds.

Weymouth parkrun is close to the beach, where there are views across to Portland and along the

Approaching the last section in Upton Country Park

Dorset Jurassic coastline. It is a flat circuitous route on a mixture of tarmac and gravel paths around Lodmoor Country Park. A walk to the beach for post-run coffee from the Top Cat café is recommended

Upton House parkrun offers a run whose spectacular scenery includes panoramic views across Holes Bay, part of Poole Harbour. It is mildly undulating and takes in some trails through woods as well as open parkland.

The Parkrun Alphabet Challenge is the goal of completing a different parkrun for every letter of the alphabet. Personal plans include getting the 'Z' out of the way by running the Ziegelweise parkrun held in Halle an der Saale, Germany. This is just over an hour by train when visiting Berlin. 'Tourist parkrunning' is a speciality in itself: whether within Dorset, the rest of the UK or further afield, it opens up the opportunity to meet a friendly group of the local community and to enjoy someone else's home parkrun. The same parkrun barcode covers all venues and will record the location and all personal race details.

France has currently suspended parkruns due to the uncertain legal situation around the requirement for a medical certificate in order to participate. This serves as a reminder that there are few guarantees in life, including the safety of going for some organised off-road exercise. Medical advice and making one's own personal multi-factorial risk assessment may minimise the risk of a critical medical incident. Risks remain. Currently work is being undertaken to provide defibrillators and training days for their use by runners at parkruns. However, the mental and physical health benefits of parkruns are well documented and provide a welcome weekly escape for many from a busy and complex world.

www.parkrun.org.uk

[The author is grateful for the warm welcome and help of all the parkrun communities he has visited in preparing this article.]

The Thomas Hardy Society

The Society's chairman, Mark Damon Chutter, reports on the year's activities

It has been a busy year for the Thomas Hardy Society. The Dorset Museum kindly asked me to deliver a lecture there during the Thomas Hardy Victorian Fair in June. Dee Tolfree, who looks after the Society's publications, also liaised with the Museum on selling some of them in the shop. Further links were also made with the Dorset History Centre and we recently held one of our council of management meetings there. Our financial situation is improving, and I would like to thank our wonderful treasurer, Lynda Kiss for everything she is doing to secure our finances. Our journal is important as it has academic gravitas, and we must make sure that our members are benefitting from all of the super events that we organise, but we must not make a loss.

Several new members have joined the council of management, and it is splendid to have new and experienced creative voices with fresh ideas.

In April we had the joint Thomas Hardy and T E Lawrence Society Study Day. A *The Return of the Native* Study Day was extremely successful and well attended. We celebrated the Birthday Weekend in June with a walk around Poundbury and Fordington and then a visit to the Keep Museum, a lecture by Brian Bates and the Mellstock Band in the evening. Sadly, we made a financial loss on this, but it was a super day. On the Sunday it was the laying of the wreath at both Stinsford and then at the statue during the Thomas Hardy Victorian Fair.

Walks around Dorchester and Wool were led by myself and Lucy Boyle-Brown respectively, one of the former being in partnership with the Dorchester Literary Festival in October. A study weekend in Swansea concerned the links between Dylan Thomas and Hardy.

Looking forward, our London Lecture will be delivered by the author of *The Chosen,* Elizabeth Lowry, in December. We then have 'Going the Rounds' in December with carols around Stinsford. In January 2024 there is the Westminster Abbey Wreath Laying Service to mark the anniversary of Hardy's death. In February we are holding a joint study weekend with the Sylvia Townsend Warner Society. April sees the *Dynasts* Study

Day. Following the Birthday Weekend, the 26th International Thomas Hardy Conference and Festival will be held in Dorchester in July. Please do come and support these events by booking on the events page of our website: www. hardysociety.org-events.

We have much to look forward to and to celebrate within our society. We now need to move forward, united in our love and passion for Hardy because that is why we are here, and Hardy connects us as that 'man who used to notice such things'.

William Barnes and the serpent

John Seymour celebrates the Ridgeway Singers and Band

The Scots will laud their darling Rabbie Burns. The Welsh have their own choral heritage, the Irish the ceilidh, Yorkshire the brass band, Cornishmen sea shanties. Geordies … no-one else speaks their language so it is impossible to know! Many other parts of these isles also strive to retain their particular ancient ways to make up the strands of our cultural warp and weft, and our own Dorset is no exception.

The Ridgeway Singers and Band were originally formed as part of the Dorset Ridgeway Landscape Partnership, supported by the Heritage Lottery Fund, with just this intention. Although this project has now ceased, the Singers and Band go from strength to strength with Dorset's own Artsreach organisation, who were also heavily involved at the outset, continuing the support which is so vital to their further success.

The initial aim of the group was to revive and secure for later generations the rich tapestry of West Gallery music, once broadly part of the common cultural life in the county. The choir is comprised of voices across the whole range and is conducted by Phil Humphries, the musical maestro of the group.

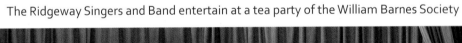

The Ridgeway Singers and Band entertain at a tea party of the William Barnes Society

Phil Humphries plays
the sinuous serpent

Tony Gill

They have mastered some complex and demanding pieces as well as those more familiar such as the enduring favourite, 'Linden Lea', the William Barnes poem set to music by Ralph Vaughan Williams. They also now incorporate a wide range of other old Dorset songs, carols and tunes together with more recent additions written by the two pivotal figures in the group, Tim Laycock and Phil. Much historical research has also been done to underpin and lend credence, validity and variety to their productions.

All such compositions are of the very fibres of the county since these two and many others are members of the William Barnes Society and, indeed, the Society of Dorset Men. These traditions inform, influence and inspire the entirety of the Singers' and Band's work. They also are an ongoing part of their efforts since accompanying the music will be several readings of the vernacular poems of William Barnes. These bring to colourful life the communities, beliefs and attitudes of that era, before the insidious effect of the railways and better roads spread the metropolitan influence and diminished the bucolic outlook, language, music and customs of this rural backwater. For an independent view of the wonders of these performances and readings, look no further than a review left on their website: 'Brilliant, uplifting singing and terrific readings – no wonder we all loved it in the audience.' With around forty singers and ten musicians, they produce a truly vibrant and joyous sound.

A video of a past performance, 'The Ridgeway Carol', written by Tim Laycock and arranged by Phil Humphries, can be seen on their website. This piece highlights the various elements of the Dorset landscape including the Bronze Age barrow called the Five Marys, Hardy's Monument above Portesham, the White King (the horse and rider cut into the chalk downs to the east of Weymouth) and the world-famous Chesil Bank. Chesil? Why, m'dear, 'tis the old Darset name for 'stony' – as in the village of Cheselbourne, ie. stony stream!

Tim Laycock with his 'squeeze box'

Since those who attend the concerts often see Phil play his new trombone, they are invariably baffled to be told that he will now also play the serpent. Some explanation is due. The serpent is a musical instrument first used in the late 1500s and is about eight feet long. It is folded into a sinuous shape (hence the name) of two connected wooden, often walnut, tubes glued together then wrapped in dark leather. Holding the instrument low down on his chest enables the sitting player to reach the mouthpiece and fingerholes. In *Under the Greenwood Tree* by Thomas Hardy, the village shoemaker, Robert Penny, describes the serpent as being 'a deep rich note'. This timbre gives a depth and substance to the overall tune in much the same way as does the tuba or bass guitar in a more modern band. There are very few in the entire country, so for a chance to see this extraordinary item, you'll have to come see the Singers! Not to be outdone, Tim Laycock airs his genuinely superb voice with his playing of the now little heard 'squeeze box' concertina, which is probably as old as most of the tunes he plays!

Concerts of their music are held throughout the county in village halls, church halls, churches and other venues too varied to mention. A visit to their website – ridgewaysingersand band.org – will allow a far wider understanding of what, why and where they are performing and enable an 'in person' appreciation of their unique contribution to our county life.

ridgewaysingersandband.org

From Sherborne to Burma
by way of Madagascar

Jeremy Archer recounts the wartime career of David Shirreff,
originally of the Dorsetshire Regiment

D avid Shirreff was born on 29 October 1919 at Naini Tal, Uttarakhand,
India, younger son of Alexander Grierson Shirreff, Indian Civil Service,
and his wife, Dulcie. Her father, Lieutenant Colonel Walter Herbert Baxter, had
commanded 1st/4th (Territorial) Battalion, Dorsetshire Regiment. He was also
the proprietor of Dorsetshire Brewery Co. (Sherborne) Ltd, and lived at The
Wilderness in Sherborne, which lay on the west side of St Swithin's Road, very
close to Long Street, but has since been redeveloped for housing.

David Shirreff attended Sherborne School and after a year at Exeter

Major A D Shirreff MC,
Dorsetshire Regiment, attached
King's African Rifles

College, Oxford, he enlisted in the Oxfordshire and Buckinghamshire Light Infantry. He never actually served in the ranks but after an interview was selected for OCTU and went straight to Sandhurst in October 1939. After four months at Sandhurst, he was commissioned into the Dorsetshire Regiment, and was initially posted to the regimental depot in Dorchester. He volunteered for a number of things to get overseas and was seconded to the King's African Rifles. It was a month's journey to Mombasa, where David joined 5th (Kenya) Battalion, King's African Rifles (5 KAR) and put in charge of a platoon. The first essential was to learn Swahili and within a month, he could just make himself understood.

5 KAR took part in the Abyssinian campaign and David Shirreff was mentioned in despatches for an assault on a dug-in Italian battalion position near Mount Fike, 75 miles south of Addis Ababa. After the Abyssinian campaign had been successfully concluded, 'We had a pet cheetah which we had found chained and manacled in the market so we bought it off this chap and it lived with us in the Mess. Eventually, when we went overseas to Madagascar, we arranged for it to be sent home to London Zoo, where it stayed until it died.'

The Madagascar operation was undertaken to prevent the Japanese moving in there: Japanese submarines were already operating in the Mozambique Channel. David's first action in the campaign was unusual: 14 Platoon was to land on Mayotte, one of the Comoro Islands, and capture the French district commissioner and whatever armed troops he had. 'I went with a small patrol to the district commissioner's house, went upstairs and found the district commissioner in bed with his 10-year-old son. The poor little chap woke up and started screaming: black-faced soldiers carrying Tommy guns at four o'clock in the morning were rather alarming. The DC was very Vichy and very hostile.'

On 25 October 1942, Lieutenant David Shirreff was recommended for – and subsequently awarded – a Military Cross for 'continuous gallantry in action'. The citation concluded: 'Throughout the whole campaign, he has shown a consistently high standard of leadership and courage, and his example has been an inspiration to all ranks.'

After the Madagascar campaign, David was promoted captain and took command of B Company, then part of the Tulear garrison in the south of the island, in May 1943. In January 1944, the battalion returned to Kenya and, after all ranks had had leave, embarked for Ceylon in July 1944. After a long journey by sea, river steamer and road, they reached Palel in Assam in September 1944. The Japanese had been defeated in the crucial battles of Kohima and Imphal and were retreating down the Kabaw Valley.

The monsoon was still at its height, which meant a muddy march of several days to join 11 Division in the Kabaw Valley, just over the border in Burma. The following month, 5 KAR were in action against a strong Japanese position at Letsegan. The Japanese were quite a different proposition from the

Soldiers of KAR having disembarked on a beach in Madagascar

Italians and the French and the battle cost the battalion about three times the casualties they had suffered in the whole of the Abyssinian campaign. David Shirreff's elder son, General Sir Richard Shirreff, wrote: 'I shall never forget attending, as a small boy, 5 KAR's Letsegan Day parade at Nanyuki in Kenya, which commemorated their proudest Burma Campaign battle honour: fine-looking, proud, immaculately-drilled Askaris in khaki, distinctive in their fezzes with their officers wearing slouch hats and brightly coloured hackles.'

After Letsegan, David Shirreff returned to B Company as company commander and 5 KAR continued to lead the 11 Division advance down the Kabaw Valley, fighting several battles to dislodge fiercely-held Japanese positions. 'I found out that you must choose between going off the track, which is slow and exhausting but one hundred per cent safe, or else going along the track, which is fast but asking for trouble if there are Japs about. The Japs, incidentally, always move along tracks, usually chattering with their rifles over their shoulders, but they don't mind being bumped off. I always moved off the tracks, largely owing to the insistence of my orderly, Private Seremon Lendioo. Very often, when I was tired of going up and down hill bending double most of the time, I would suggest going onto the track, but my orderly always refused to let me. In fact, he really commanded all my patrols.'

B Company had to cross over the Chindwin and take over from the Assam Regiment, who were already across: 'We started crossing on rafts made of grass and tarpaulins, which were unwieldy and rather dangerous. The first attempt to carry mules resulted in a mule losing its head, kicking out wildly and knocking the crew into the water. One Askari was run down by the rescue launch and drowned. The mule swam back to the shore. After that we gave up the idea of taking mules across. At midday an airdrop produced collapsible assault boats, which were a great improvement. All B Company was across by the evening, which was not a bad achievement as the river was over 1000 yards wide, the current strong, and the Askaris' idea of navigation very rudimentary.'

A little more than three weeks after crossing the Chindwin, B Company was ordered to attack a Japanese position and, if possible, capture it, otherwise to do as much damage as possible and then withdraw. David was crossing a small ravine when 'a Jap on the other side threw two grenades at me. I was hit in the right arm and back and my orderly was badly wounded. The Japs were clinging tenaciously to their final position, it was getting dark and we were short of ammunition. I explained the situation to the CO over the wireless, and

The Chindwin river

David Shirreff's Samburu orderly, Private Seremon Lendioo, with David's children. After the war, he would regularly arrive unannounced from his tribal lands in the Northern Frontier district of Kenya to wherever David was posted, and stay for a few weeks before returning to his wives and cattle.

asked for more ammunition and another company to complete the job. If I had not been wounded myself, I might have put in another attack, but I did not want to leave others to do what I certainly did not relish myself, so I was quite grateful when the CO ordered a withdrawal.

'I was beginning to feel rather weedy and my right arm was useless, but I could walk well enough. We set off carrying our loot. In the darkness, platoons were separated but we all eventually arrived at our dump. Next morning, the doctor took me and the other wounded down to the Brigade Field Ambulance. As there was no landing ground in operation at that time, we could not be evacuated until the bridgehead was joined up, so we lay for a week on stretchers under parachute tents. I was quite comfortable but very bored as there was nothing to read. The battalion went on down to the main Yeu road and remained in the forefront until the bridgehead was finally linked up and 2 Division passed through. B Company was forward company most of the time and did more than its share of the work. Yet when 2 Division passed through, the Askaris did not want to go back and rest. They wanted to go forward and finish the job and then be allowed to go back to Africa.'

After the war, David Shirreff joined the Colonial Service and served as a district officer and district commissioner in Kenya. Following Kenyan independence on 1 June 1963, he returned to England, qualified as a solicitor, settled near Bury St Edmunds and became a partner in a local firm of solicitors. Described in his obituary in the *Daily Telegraph* as 'a modest, courageous and talented man' and 'a keen ornithologist, an enthusiastic fox hunter and devoted countryman', David Shirreff died on 12 July 1999.

1st Battalion The Rifles 2022-2023

1st Battalion The Rifles is the linear descendant of the Dorsetshire Regiment. Captain Jonathan Cox gives a taste of some of its recent activities

In September 2022, 1st Battalion The Rifles completed Exercise Askari Storm in the gruelling heat of Kenya: infantry manoeuvres using simulated ammunition, complex live firing ranges, community engagement, and some of the best adventurous training the Army has to offer.

In February, 1 Rifles conducted a Junior Non-Commissioned Officer course in Okehampton, Dartmoor. The prospect of conducting this arduous course was daunting, but many Riflemen volunteered to have themselves tested and proved. With 21 days in the field, each with a steady but relentless tempo which really stretched the students, those who passed the course are as prepared as possible to lead Riflemen.

'No one will faint; there is no room for independent thought,' barked the General Officer Commanding London District as the orders for the Coronation concluded in the splendid Guards Chapel. We were about to see the Army demonstrate its most traditional values – displaying its might in honour of the King. Despite a busy spring, a team from the 1st and 7th Battalions had been put through their paces and had managed to impress the Foot Guards enough to progress to the next stage.

Every day saw an average of 25,000 steps and 4500 calories: more akin to the Roman legionnaires than modern physical training. Aching feet and backs were soon forgotten in the extreme pageantry of the day

The Junior NCO Course on Dartmoor

itself, 6 May. Dive in and let the training carry you through, and experience real enjoyment as your regimental contingent gets to show off to the millions of spectators, marching to its spot in Whitehall. Then the long wait until the Coronation concludes and the whole parade steps off together, with all nineteen bands striking up simultaneously.

Along Pall Mall and into the gardens of Buckingham Palace. Shoulder to shoulder, everyone waits for their Majesties to arrive. The national anthem plays, and then it's hats off for the loudest three cheers you can manage. And suddenly, you're extremely proud to be British, and serving in the best armed forces in the world, and in the finest regiment at that.

On 18 May 1 Rifles paraded through Chepstow. The parade gave the battalion the opportunity to say farewell and thank the town for fifteen years of hospitality and assistance, ahead of the move to Cyprus. The parade saw the battalion march down the High Street, where they saluted HRH The Duke of Kent. The people of Chepstow turned up in strength, with lots of well-wishers and even a promise of a leaving party from Pitchers, the local nightclub!

Potentially the most difficult thing the battalion has achieved is an entire unit move to Cyprus during the summer. It took a month as almost 1000 people – Riflemen, wives, husbands and children – moved to Cyprus with countless bags and boxes in tow. The battalion also moved truckloads of equipment to set up our new home. 1 Rifles are very much enjoying their first few weeks of their two-year stay in Cyprus, immersing themselves in the culture and beauty of the island, but there is a quiet and unspoken longing for our home back in England.

www.army.mod.uk/who-we-are/corps-regiments-and-units/infantry/the-rifles/regular-rifles/

Representatives of The Rifles who took part in Operation Golden Orb: the Coronation.

The William Barnes Society

Brian Caddy and Devina Symes report on the Society's busy year

It has been another busy and enjoyable year for the William Barnes Society, with members enjoying a varied programme of events.

Our Christmas celebration of 'Keepen up o' Christmas' was a lively and happy evening, where members were entertained with festive poems and music, followed by tea and mince pies.

Our 2023 programme began on 23 April with the Annual Service of Remembrance and Thanksgiving for the life of William Barnes at St Peter's church, Winterborne Came. The church was packed for the service, which was taken by Rev. Anthony Bush. Members of the Society read dialect poems during the service, and Jane Ashdown and Jill Bryant gave the Old and New Testament readings respectively. Following the service, wreaths were laid on the graves of William and Laura Barnes by Society members David and Susan Guy.

21 May was sunny and dry for the Society's visit to Mere. As we assembled in the Grove Building, we were greeted by tea and home-made biscuits, along with a friendly welcome, by the Friends of St Michael's Church. Following a welcome from Janet Way, who had kindly organised the day, the chairman, Brian Caddy, gave a short talk on 'Barnes at Mere', concluding with the eclogue, 'The Common a-Took in', for which Godfrey Symes joined him. Devina Symes then read 'To a Garden on Leaving It'. This was followed by a short walk around Mere, led by Janet, who pointed out the many interesting places which were Barnes-related.

Following lunch, we all made our way to Chantry House where, by the kind invitation of Mr and Mrs Wilson, we wandered freely around the peaceful garden. After we had taken in the beauty of this peaceful spot, the local choir formed a semi-circle to sing 'Linden Lea' for us, which was magical. The day closed back at the Grove Building, where the Friends of St Michael's were waiting to serve us tea and home-made cakes. Everyone agreed that it had been a most interesting and happy day.

Our summer talk was given by Society member John Blackmore on 10 June at St George's Hall, Fordington. The well-researched and interesting talk,

which was interspersed with some of John's songs from his CD, 'The Beauty of Blackmore', was about William Barnes and the role of other regional writers in 19th-century nation-building.

On 5 July, by courtesy of Morag and George Titley, the society enjoyed a most happy and enjoyable summer tea at Came House. The afternoon began with Colin and Ruth Thompson and Tim Laycock playing some delightful folk tunes, then there was a surprise visit from William Barnes (aka Peter Allison), who regaled us with memories of the folk who lived at Came during his time as the parson there. Barnes was surprised when a village lady from his time (Joy Parsons) appeared, and they both recited 'A Bit o' Sly Coortin'. More readings and music followed before a most delicious high tea, courtesy of Joy and David Parsons, was served by them and their helper, Diane.

At the Oak Fayre at Stock Gaylard on 27 August, members assembled in the church on the estate to read the poetry of William Barnes. As we were at the Oak Fayre, the theme was 'Trees', a subject about which Barnes wrote profusely.

On 15 September, as part of Heritage Week, members provided readings and music in Whitcombe church, where William Barnes became a curate in 1847. The event was followed by a tea kindly provided by Alec and Minette Walters.

The final event was the annual celebration of William Barnes at Max Gate, the home of Thomas Hardy. The event was organised by Tim Laycock and friends, who provided readings and music.

New members are always welcome to the William Barnes Society, and for all news, events and photographs, please visit the William Barnes website: www.williambarnessociety.org.uk.

Art and alchemy

John Seymour has visited Langham's Wine Estate

Those not intimately aware of just what it takes to establish, literally from the ground up, a thriving and growing wine estate would do well to visit Langham's Winery, near the village of Dewlish in the south of the county. Should there be any surprise at the production of fine wines here, it is particularly relevant that the extensive remains of a Roman villa are a stone's throw away on the edge of these green acres, for it is well known that the Romans grew and produced wines in just this area's climate and soils.

The driving personality and vision in this era is that of a local farmer turned viticulturist, Justin Langham. Intrigued by visits to New World vineyards on family holidays with his father, John, when the need arose for his traditional farming to diversify into other activities less subject to economic fluctuations, he hit upon the prospect of wine production. Much research followed and Justin toured many of the world's most famous wine regions

before studying viticulture at Plumpton College. Thorough investigations into the viability of such a venture identified four possible locations, which were then subject to professional assessment by others. That resulted in the business being sited in the largely derelict buildings at Crawthorne Farm, which gave an invaluable collection of barns and

Justin Langham

Where it all begins

structures plus the geographical position of the fields and, crucially, the terroir – the soil type on which the whole venture would be based.

With a south-facing aspect and chalk soils, Crawthorne Vinyard provides the perfect setting for growing and ripening the grapes. Established hedgerows and mature trees shield the whole site from the prevailing south-westerly winds and allow a large variety of beneficial organisms to flourish. Constant attention to reduce even the small amount of chemical usage is enabled by careful vine canopy management, and disease impact is lessened by the increased air flow that this generates. Free from the constraints of contract purchasing, the crop can then be picked at optimum ripeness, resulting in a far better quality of wine.

The initial years of any such undertaking are invariably fraught since a lot of front-end investment is necessary, while any production and income is a few years hence, after saleable wines have been produced – subject to the weather and Mother Nature. From a tenuous start in 2009, when just 30 acres were planted, to a further 45 in 2022, the tide of vines and wines has risen. It will rise by another 10 acres in 2024, centred around the Champagne varieties, since Langham's mainly produce a sparkling wine of Chardonnay, Pinot Noir and Pinot Meunier.

It doesn't end there, however, and this is where the art element becomes vital. Depending on the style of wine you are aiming for, then the root stock on which the type of vine is grafted has a fundamental role in many aspects of the final item. As just the beginning, you may choose the French preference of a short graft or the German of a long graft. Each has particular qualities and there are a complex series of sub-divisions to decide. It's no place for anyone without an extensive knowledge of these intricacies.

There is very much an all-embracing traditional philosophy throughout the entire operation, which permeates the approach and attitudes from the top down. It runs even through the picking, since they take every bunch by hand. With the winery located within metres of the vines, the grapes are picked and processed within a few hours, which avoids the need to transport them over any distance and so compromise the quality. Finings are not used to settle the wine, nor are the wines filtered – techniques common to the larger producer – since that would alter the fundamental flavours. Storage is in a temperature-controlled environment where a mix of used traditional oak barrels, mainly from Burgundy and Bordeaux, and stainless steel tanks holds the many litres of new and ageing

Traditional oak barrels are used for storage

product. As with Champagne, they use only the traditional method to produce the sparkle, utilising a second, in-bottle fermentation to do so. Each bottle is then aged for a further 18 months on naturally produced yeast lees before being disgorged and aged further under new natural corks.

The blending of wine from these classic types depends on one man with a most subtle and experienced nose and palate. Hence the alchemy! He will ensure that each year is as close to their standard as possible, although Nature will ensure small variations. This individual is Tommy. After a season of labelling and bottling wine as a summer job, he worked at Sharpham Vineyard in Devon before joining the Langham team in January 2019 as assistant winemaker to Daniel Ham. In the next January he took the reins to become head winemaker and is committed to continuing and developing the ethos of minimal intervention in the entire natural process.

Plainly, the burgeoning business will soon outgrow the current facilities and other more specific buildings will follow. The number of those working with Justin — currently three full-time and three part-time in the vineyards, five others in the winery, plus a good few during harvest — will also increase.

langhamwine.co.uk

Upsydown

Some lighter moments provided by Lyndon Wall, an award-winning Dorset cartoonist whose work regularly appears in publications around the county (including the *Dorset Year Book* 2022 and 2023)

It was my dad, himself a talented studio potter, who instructed me from an early age in the art of painting and drawing. Observation of form and texture, light and shadow, the judicious use of colour – all were key, as was practice, endless practice.

As a schoolboy I remember the thrill of gaining my Blue Peter Badge, coming runner-up in their national painting competition (26,000 entries), and then being taken on by an agent, producing greetings card illustrations and advertising signs for London department stores. The advertising signs required almost no creative input but needed to be painted quickly and accurately: useful grounding for live caricature drawing (which I still do), where a finished likeness is produced inside five minutes.

During the 1990s I used to draw black and white caption cartoons for various London journals using the old Letraset shading dots. About five years ago, a newly-launched Dorset magazine took me on. Further local publications followed, accepting both political and Dorset-themed cartoons. This in turn led to an exciting moment: coming runner-up to The Sun in the national Ellwood Atfield Political Cartoon of The Year Awards 2022.

www.justsocaricatures.co.uk

The legendary Queen guitarist and wildlife campaigner, Sir Brian May, bought 157 acres of farmland near Bere Regis back in 2012. It is steadily being restored to natural woodland to promote wildlife, and is open to the public.

A curious incident made local news a few years ago. A pile of clothes was discovered on Weymouth beach, triggering responses from the emergency services. Through a mobile phone found among the items, the owner was traced to a nearby pub. But wearing what? The story reminded me of a similar episode in the iconic 1970s sitcom, *The Fall and Rise of Reginald Perrin*, which featured Leonard Rossiter as Reggie and John Barron as his overbearing boss, CJ.

Larcombe's of Beaminster celebrates twenty successful years in the ironmongery business. The current owner of the family-run business, Simon Larcombe, looks happy to be flanked by the two Ronnies, Corbett and Barker, and Trigger from *Only Fools and Horses.*

The former World War II underground transmitter bunker on the Jurassic Coast near Weymouth has been brought back to life for holiday lettings: a great excuse to have the cast of *Dad's Army* in temporary residence.

Back in 2022 there was a fundraising appeal for the restoration of the historic (1683) faceless clock in Yetminster church. This seemed a good reason for imagining the much-loved Dorset folk group, the Yetties (who had actually retired in 2011), busking for the cause.

[Upsydown: Cartoons of Dorset Life, a book of Lyndon Wall's cartoons, will be published in May 2024 by Amberley Publishing]

In the front line

Barbara Cossins is a member of a Dorset farming dynasty and founder of Love Local Trust Local

The Cossins family have been here in the Tarrant Valley since 1877 and have been wholesale milk suppliers since 1910. The dairy herd achieved pedigree status back in 1915, which we are still proud to have to this day. We are a large working farming family who are still actively involved in running the farm as well as a butchery and farm shop. So welcome to Rawston Farm, surrounded by Cranborne Chase, an area of outstanding natural beauty. The farm is nestled

Jim Riggs driving a Fordson tractor with a Minneapolis Moline trailer bagger combine, with Ernest Cossins (third generation) taking off bags, 1949

in the beautiful Tarrant Valley to the east of Blandford Forum, with natural lush and mineral-rich grass and with the River Tarrant, a 12-km-long tributary of the River Stour, running through it.

Rawston Farm is a predominantly traditional mixed farm, approximately 2500 acres (1012 hectares), of which 1600 acres (647 hectares) are owned by the family with the rest being a combination of rented and contract farming. We have 300 milking cows across two herds, mainly Friesian Holstein, and keep 180 head of cattle, including traditional breeds such as Aberdeen Angus and Herefords, which go into the farm's butchery and shop that we opened in 2012.

Above: The little water wheel house, built by Ernest Cossins, is to this day working to provide water to the animals

Below: James Cossins (fifth generation) checking over his herd of milking cows, 2023

We also grow 1800 acres (728 hectares) of crops including winter barley, winter wheat, spring barley, spring beans, oilseed and maize.

We are proud of our roots and are now six generations with farming experience, which is in itself a real achievement (with a seventh generation in the making, only 17 months old and wanting to read only *Farmers Weekly*). All the Cossins have been forward-thinking and achieving in their own ways, working hard to maintain their family farm, working the land to provide for their families and working with a business that has evolved over many decades.

We have seen many changes in farming during those decades, in machinery, technologies, employees and much more. Yet the challenges that we face now are mind-boggling. For example, we are in a nitrate water catchment area, because we are in the heart of the Tarrant Valley, so we have to adjust our farming methods with the amount of fertilisers and be very careful of ground water leaching into the river, as well as needing to address our net zero emissions. We are in the front line of the battle to strike a balance between caring for our environment but also producing food rather than importing it thousands of miles from the other side of the world.

Back in 1993 we bought the local pub, the Langton Arms, which we have been running for 30 years. It has won many awards over the years under the Cossins family ownership, but on one awful night in 2004, disaster struck and the pub burnt down from a chimney fire which destroyed the business and the building. We worked hard over many years to rebuild and recover but sadly, the fire seems easy to deal with compared to the number of challenges we are facing today.

In 2018, at Open Farm Sunday, many people were saying that they didn't know what to trust any more thanks to things like the horsemeat scandal, fake farms in the supermarkets, and imported cheap food being rewrapped and repackaged under the British flag, so the Cossins family decided that they needed to make a stand against the misleading food labelling industry and created a label, Love Local Trust Local, for the public to know what was grown and produced in their own 30-mile radius. In 2020 we also launched the

Love Local Trust Local food awards to celebrate small independent businesses that needed help and the feeling of being part of something in these very challenging times. It was a label created by farmers for farmers, fishermen and food producers, to showcase everything that is grown, produced, caught, reared, brewed, crafted or cooked here in Dorset.

We are now going into our fourth year of awards. We feel that need to support new and small businesses, especially as there is little support out there at the moment for growing food in our own country. We should be proud to support what we produce right here in Dorset, as we British farmers have the highest standards in the world.

When farming is in your blood, you keep going because it's your business, your home and your life. We know nothing else; despite the challenges, we love what we do and when you still have young people that are following you and want to farm for the future, it's a joyous journey.

Love Local Trust Local: www.lovelocaltrustlocalawards.co.uk
Rawston Farm Butchery: www.rawstonfarmbutchery.co.uk
The Langton Arms: www.thelangtonarms.co.uk

An aerial view of the cleared site

Finding Wimborne All Hallows church

Vanessa Joseph reports on an important archaeological
investigation in East Dorset

It all started with a poem written and posted online by Terry Yarrow, aka The
Dorset Rambler. The poem, reproduced at the end of this article, ultimately
led to the re-discovery of the 'lost' church of Wimborne All Hallows (also known
as All Saints), north-west of Wimborne St Giles in East Dorset. The hamlet of
Wimborne All Hallows is in the chalklands of Cranborne Chase, a landscape
renowned for its archaeological features from all periods of human history,
with many from prehistoric times. The church was located on a spur of land
overlooking the River Allen, on a site still defined by ancient yew trees and near
a spring. The nature of the site suggests a pre-Christian origin. The church was
systematically demolished in the early 18th century before a church was rebuilt

closer to the manor house at Wimborne St Giles. The All Hallows churchyard continued to be used for burials up to the beginning of the 20th century. Today, it is still consecrated ground.

Peter Shand, a member of the public, read the poem and visited the overgrown and deserted graveyard. At that point it was a wooded glade revered locally for its annual display of snowdrops and other wildflowers. Inspired by its special qualities and atmosphere, Peter volunteered his services to the Wimborne St Giles parochial church council (PCC). The offer to clear the undergrowth was eagerly accepted, but he was also asked to contact a local historical society to investigate the history of the site further and to find evidence of the lost church. In 2020, Peter contacted the East Dorset Antiquarian Society (EDAS), a volunteer-led charity committed to the exploration, excavation, recording and conservation of archaeological monuments and antiquities. The EDAS trustees agreed to run a project on behalf of the PCC.

The Domesday Book refers to a settlement or farm named Opewinburne or Obpe Winborna, and the first mention of a church is in 1291 in the Taxatio Ecclesiastica (church valuations). The parish of Wymborn was divided in 1298, with half being given to the Abbess of the Convent of Tarent (Tarrant Crawford Abbey) and the rest shared between Lords Matravers and Fitzalan. Later, during the Dissolution (1539), all assets were passed back to the Crown and re-united.

In 1651, Sir Anthony Ashley Cooper, 1st Earl of Shaftesbury, re-built

the manor house close to Wimborne St Giles. In 1732, with permission from George II, the 4th Earl of Shaftesbury consolidated All Hallows parish with that at Wimborne St Giles. Shortly afterwards, the church at Wimborne All Hallows was demolished, leaving the graveyard.

The project was quite an undertaking as it was the time of Covid and Government guidelines restricted outdoor activities to six people on a site at the same time. Fortunately, desk research could be done from home. Key objectives included locating the church, defining its footprint, determining the structure of the building and considering the site in relationship to the landscape. EDAS undertook to locate and record as many graves as possible, to create a site map featuring all monuments and structural components, to research the history of the church and its relationship with other churches in the area, and to explore historical records about the families buried on the site. We were asked to avoid graves, respect human and structural remains, leave the site as found – and try not to lose the snowdrops.

In autumn 2020, between lockdowns, volunteers surveyed the churchyard, clearing and mapping the site and its boundaries, probing for lost grave markers, and photographing and recording individual gravestones. We also put in small trenches to try to locate the building remains, and two corners and some small sections of the church walls were revealed.

The earliest remaining marker was a ledger stone for Edmund Laurence, Gent, from 1680; the latest was for Frederick Bartlett in 1925. Most of the burials were from the 19th century, although a small number of grave slabs were uncovered dating from the 17th and early 18th centuries, predating the demolition of the church. It is likely that some of the later burials were deliberately positioned within the footprint of the demolished church.

Left and right: EDAS members excavating and recording the site

The most impressive tomb was that of Henry and Harriet Lowry-Corry. Harriet was the daughter of the 6th Earl of Shaftesbury and her husband, Henry Thomas Lowry-Corry, was the son of the 2nd Earl of Belmore, an Irish title. This magnificent tomb contained a major mason's error with two Es in THE; it was one of several mason's mistakes we noted.

Other grave markers revealed stories of unfortunate and accidental deaths. John Rideout died in 1862 from injuries he received 'by a waggon running over him, aged 58 years'. Prudence Barfoot of Woodlands, aged 12 years, belonged to St Giles National School, where her death on 24 April 1829 was 'occasioned by her clothes catching fire'.

The EDAS team returned to Wimborne All Hallows in the summer of 2021. Now, our objective was to reveal the footprint of the demolished building and gather evidence of how it had been constructed. Peter Shand cleared the site again! Just like Time Team, we had a deadline: five weeks to find the church. To everyone's delight, we succeeded in locating the footprint, exposing lengths of the west, south and east walls, including three corners. We hoped to find evidence of a tower. We found it on the last day of the dig!

As an amateur society, EDAS actively engages with the public and local communities, encouraging an interest in local history through research and

The footprint of the church revealed. Later graves have infringed on the space.

archaeological investigation and inviting them to share our passion for archaeology. During the dig, we spoke to many members of the local community as they walked their dogs or wandered past. The Earl of Shaftesbury visited us on a couple of occasions. We organised Open Days to share our findings with the local community and other EDAS members. More than a hundred people visited the site and £113

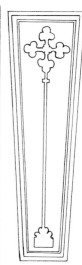

The medieval cross slab

was raised for the St Giles Roof Appeal. People shared childhood memories of playing among the graves. Several families enjoyed guided tours.

At the end of the five weeks, the site was backfilled and EDAS volunteers replanted the snowdrop bulbs which had been carefully collected during the excavation. Peace descended once more on the graveyard at All Hallows, but not before we had established that the church of Wimborne All Hallows was a two-cell structure with well-built flint walls and greensand ashlar quoins, typical of churches in the Cranborne Chase area. The tower was positioned to the north of the nave and the differences in construction suggest it was added later, perhaps in the 16th century.

The roof was mainly ceramic tiles, with lower rows of limestone, similar to the church at Tarrant Crawford and other local churches. Fragments of glazed ridge tiles in red, greens and amber indicate that the exterior was decorated in an attractive style. Several fragments of medieval floor tiles were found with 'Wessex style' designs, like those found in Shaftesbury Abbey, Milton Abbey and Tarrant Crawford Abbey. Only 23 out of 140 medieval parish churches in Dorset were known to have inlaid floor tiles.

Post-excavation examination of the finds, including pottery, glass fragments, coins and building materials, all pointed to a church with 12th- and 13th-century origins. The fact that finds were limited is evidence of systematic dismantling of the fabric and contents of the church to remove anything of value.

Probably the most important document we found, post-excavation, is held in the Bodleian Library in Oxford and includes sketches by Browne Willis (1682-1760), an antiquarian and friend of John Hutchins. These were apparently done after the demolition of Wimborne All Hallows church and a few aspects don't fully accord with the archaeology. However, his plan aligns closely with what EDAS discovered and the elevation added to our knowledge by showing that there was a short spire on the tower.

During the excavation, an unusual Purbeck marble coffin-shaped slab was uncovered, from a 13th-century burial. The medieval cross slab was located close to the foundations of the south wall of the nave, the preferred place for important burials. During the 1200s, it would have been a prestigious and expensive monument commemorating a person of status and wealth well known to the community. At that period there were no inscriptions and unfortunately, no records have been found which give us a clue about the buried individual. Tantalising remains of other marble slabs pointed to more than one high-status burial at the church in medieval times.

The cross slab from Wimborne All Hallows has been reburied. However, it is significant for the unusual points of detail in its carving and for its completeness and state of preservation. Its discovery and recording by EDAS

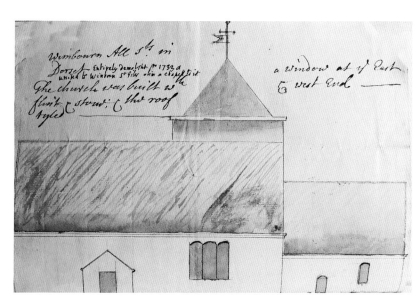

One of the Browne Willis sketches

and experts in the field adds to the corpus of knowledge of these medieval monuments.

In October 2022, we reconvened in St Giles village hall to present our findings. These included research into individuals buried in the graveyard as well as discoveries about the church itself. The hall was packed – apparently the largest audience there ever. When the post-excavation work has been completed, we will provide the local community with material for a guidebook. EDAS will also prepare a paper for publication in the *Proceedings of the Dorset Natural History and Archaeological Society*.

Finally, a note on the date of the new church at Wimborne St Giles. Lord Shaftesbury's letter to the 'Lord Keeper of the Great Seal' in 1684, petitioning to unite Wimborne All Hallows with Wimborne St Giles, states that the people of Allhallowes 'all come to St. Gyleses church the other having long layen ruined'. This letter was transcribed by Allan Cooper for a *Dorset Year Book* article entitled 'Hard up in Dorset' in the 1975/76 edition. New research of parish registers, now available on Ancestry, shows no indication of this movement away from Wimborne All Hallows, nor of its ruinous state.

Allan Cooper also stated that the church at Wimborne St Giles was rebuilt in 1732, a year before the Wimborne All Hallows church was demolished. It is likely that this date came from Hutchins's *History & Antiquities of the County of Dorset*, which states (under Wimborne St Giles church): 'the church and tower were rebuilt, 1732, soon after Wimborne All Saints was annexed.' Nikolaus Pevsner gives the same date in the *Dorset* volume of *The Buildings of England*.

However, EDAS has found evidence in the parish registers of continuous marriages through 1732 and up to 7 January 1738, then a gap until the next marriage on 15 December 1743, so it looks likely that the new church at Wimborne St Giles was not completed until 1743.

Who Cares?
by Terry Yarrow (The Dorset Rambler)

Faceless names upon the stone,
No one knows, they are gone,
Ashes to ashes, no-one there,
Does anyone care?
Loved ones once, when alive,
But all too soon, their time to die,
Leaving this earth, with mourners there,
People around to care!
Generations passed, all forgot,
No-one now tends their final plot,
Overgrown and in disrepair,
Does anyone care?
Who cares?

[The East Dorset Antiquarian Society (EDAS) is an amateur society which actively engages with the public and local communities, inviting you to share our passion for archaeology through a varied programme of activities.

EDAS activities include: monthly lectures from September to May each year; fieldwork and excavations directed by EDAS; field trips researched and organised by members to look at history and archaeology in other areas of the UK; guided walks and outings to places of interest in Dorset and neighbouring counties; and a regular newsletter to keep members informed of local and wider topics in archaeology and history. Practical archaeology remains at the centre of our activities. EDAS offers members of all ages the opportunity to gain field experience and acquire new skills in excavation and post-excavation work. Members of the EDAS Committee engage with a range of professionals in the field and prepares detailed reports on excavations for publication.

EDAS was founded in 1983 and is a registered charity.
www.dorset-archaeology.org.uk.]

Book review

The Keep in 60 People,
edited by Christopher Jary.

Review by Peter Lush

In 2021 I reviewed *The Keep in 50 Objects* and questioned how you choose such a small number from the 80,000 available. Christopher Jary and his team have now produced *The Keep in 60 People*. It follows the same format and poses the same question. Here, however, the subjects, although bound together by their service in one of the seven regiments represented at the Keep Military Museum, are chosen often as much for their civilian achievements as for their military prowess.

It is easy to forget that lurking behind a military uniform and a rigid discipline are human beings with lives as diverse as anyone could imagine. Here is the Viscount who enlisted as a private soldier, the farm labourer's son who left school at twelve but became managing director of Vauxhall Motors, the stable lad who volunteered to serve as his master's batman – but don't let me spoil it for you. This book belongs on your coffee table, where you can digest each two-page biography at will and at leisure. The story of the NAAFI manager who was decorated for bravery in the Falklands points vividly to the fact that whatever is achieved in civilian employment has often been enabled by military training and experience.

There is another thread that binds this book. Each choice has been made and written by a volunteer at the Keep and it is their diligence and devotion in the care of the memory of these outstanding men that keeps them at the forefront of our conscience. May our county and our country continue to produce citizens of such calibre.

[*The Keep in 60 People* is available only from the Keep. It can be ordered from their on-line shop at www.keepmilitarymuseum.org/shop or by post from The Keep Military Museum, Barrack Road, Dorchester DT1 1RN. Each copy costs £15 including postage.]

'The finest armoured vehicle museum in the world'

Jeremy Pope celebrates the Tank Museum's centenary

The Tank Museum marked its centenary in June 2023, when the Duke of Kent, its Patron, visited to dedicate a Memorial Room for those who had served in the Royal Armoured Corps, and to celebrate the centenary itself. Dorset can also celebrate and take pride in the amazing asset that was established, it is said, following a visit to Bovington in 1923 by Rudyard Kipling, who suggested that the many vehicles which had been returned to Bovington after the Great War should be preserved. The tank as an armoured fighting vehicle had been developed during that war at, it is said, the behest of Winston Churchill, to overcome the problems presented by trench warfare, enabling armoured vehicles to attack the enemy across the somewhat static boundaries of the front lines.

Those vehicles that returned to Bovington, along with the original prototypes such as Little Willie, were assembled in a shed that was to become

The Tank Museum was established 100 years ago as a technical and teaching collection to support both the mechanical and weapons training of tank soldiers

On his visit to celebrate the Museum's centenary, HRH The Duke of Kent dedicated a Memorial Room for those who had served in the Royal Armoured Corps. The Tank Museum is the museum of both the Royal Armoured Corps and the Royal Tank Regiment and tells the stories of British soldiers who have served in armoured fighting vehicles. It is also a place of memorial and commemoration, where visitors are invited to remember the sacrifice which is an inevitable consequence of conflict.

the Museum. Vehicles were added to the collection as they came out of service or trials and experiments concluded. Other tank-related memorabilia were collected and an archive and library begun, but it was not until 1947 that the Museum really began to develop, when the current WW2 Hall was used as the Museum and opened to the general public. In that year about 2500 people visited. Today that figure has increased nearly a hundredfold for actual visitors, and to almost unimaginable numbers when virtual visitors are added.

From these basic foundations the Museum has undergone a remarkable expansion, which began in 1981 with the arrival of George Forty as Curator. Vehicles were obtained, mainly through exchange with other museums or as gifts, from all over the world. George began work on the restoration of vehicles within the collection, and in 1984 a small conservation workshop was established. In 1990/92 the first purpose-built workshop was constructed, the workshop staff numbers grew and their number was augmented by involving volunteers in their work, which has been key to its continued success.

The Tank Museum welcomes over 200,000 visitors from this country and overseas to view the world's biggest collection of military armoured vehicles

Since that time the Museum has undergone a series of developments to enable it to conserve and display its growing collection of vehicles, as well as its expanding archive. During the latter part of the 20th century, projects included the construction of the British Steel Hall over part of the car park, the Tamiya Hall and an improved entrance hall and reception, enabling the Museum to cope with the arrival of new exhibits. This was particularly so following the Gulf War in 1991, with the addition of captured Iraqi vehicles, mainly of Soviet and Chinese origin.

In addition, in 1998 a new immersive experience was created in the Trench Experience, which enabled visitors to see and understand what trench warfare was all about rather than simply looking at tanks. It was the first development to focus not just on the tanks themselves but also on the people who fought in them and against them, by telling the story of the first tank crews. Not surprisingly, it has remained hugely popular and was refreshed in 2016. Much credit must go to John Woodward, who had taken over the role of Curator and Director of the Museum in September 1993.

John was also responsible for the next major programme to transform the Museum, with his approach to the Heritage Lottery Fund that enabled the re-development of the entrance, shop, café and a huge new display hall: the Tank Story Hall or, as it is also known, the Woodward Hall. The overall cost of the project amounted to £16m, of which the HLF provided £9.6m with the remainder being raised by the Museum and support from a number of charitable funds. The display in the hall tells the story of the tank from its invention during World War 1 with Little Willie and its subsequent development through to World War 2 and up to the present day. It shows that sequence of development, not only in this country but across the world, through fascinating items such as the 'swimming' Sherman tanks used on D-Day for the invasion of Normandy, as well as many features about those who fought in and against the various exhibits.

For example, one of these tells the story of how the Tiger Tank, which is now a major vehicle in the Museum's running fleet, was disabled and captured in North Africa.

Having started the project, John retired in 2006 and was succeeded by Richard Smith, the first Director to be recruited from a non-military background. He has built on and driven forward the performance, reputation and financial stability of this remarkable Dorset asset. From the opening of the Woodward Hall by HM Queen Elizabeth II in June 2009 to the present, the development of the Museum has proceeded apace. In 2013 the Vehicle Conservation Centre was built to enable the collection to be properly stored and conserved, where previously too many vehicles had been parked outside. Then in May 2018 a new workshop was opened by the Princess Royal. This has consolidated the restoration of vehicles, especially the running fleet, which are critical for the displays in the arena.

Alongside these physical developments, huge progress has been made with regular refreshing of the displays, to stimulate continued interest in what is on view. For example, thematic re-displays have included 'Battlegroup Afghanistan', much of which was put together by members of the Army who had served in Afghanistan. Interestingly, this was visited by many families of personnel who took part in the conflict so that they could understand what their relatives had experienced, down even to temporary accommodation and catering. In so doing, it proved a cathartic experience. Other re-displays have included 'Warhorse to Horsepower', covering the transition of cavalry regiments from their mounts to armoured vehicles.

The interior view of the Tank Museum's Vehicle Conservation Centre. The VCC houses over 100 armoured fighting vehicles, including a wide variety of unique prototypes and testbed vehicles.

The Tank Museum's workshop was opened in 2018 by Princess Anne and allows the engineering team to preserve and restore the vehicles in the Museum's collection

The Tank Museum attracts more than 26,000 visitors over the annual three-day Tankfest, the Tank Museum's flagship fundraising event

The Tank Museum's latest exhibition, 'Tanks for the Memories', explores the story of the tank as a cultural icon and marks the centenary of the establishment of the Tank Museum. Highlights include the Museum's Sherman Fury tank, which was the star of the 2014 Hollywood film, *Fury*, as well as items from the Tank Museum's involvement in *War Horse* and Indiana Jones films.

Displays of vehicles from the Museum's collection take place regularly and are a great attraction to visitors. These displays provide the spectacle of tanks actually operating, in addition to the static displays, and advanced by leaps and bounds when, as part of the redevelopment opened in 2009, the Kuwait Arena was constructed. Special events have been added to the programme, including Tiger Days and, of course, Tankfest, held at the end of June for three days. In 2023 it attracted a record 26,000 visitors from all over the world to help celebrate the Museum's centenary; in addition, over 60,000 online tank fans watched the display.

Perhaps the most impressive development has been the way in which the Museum has evolved its online audiences alongside the onsite activities already described. Working in close collaboration with Wargaming, a major video game company, it can now boast that the online audience reached over 90 million people on YouTube and TikTok in 2022. The online audience tends to be more expert than the onsite audience, as it provides them with a wide range of information in which they already have an interest. The Museum regards this area as having huge potential.

However, the Museum's collections are at the heart of all it does. Its purpose is to use these collections to tell the story of tanks and the people serving with them. But in so doing, it addresses a wide variety of audiences through a number of touch points.

It is more than 20 years since I became involved as a Trustee of the Museum and I count myself very fortunate to have seen its transformation from a tin hut, with lots of metal inside and even more outside, just about breaking even financially, to such a vibrant, interesting and impressive enterprise. Museums are usually regarded as rather dry and boring, which is the last thing one could say about the Tank Museum. It is a varied and amazing body with so many facets. It is a shrine to commemorate those who served in the Royal Armoured Corps, who fought in and against tanks and who lived and died in the service in so many conflicts around the world during the last century, and their comradeship; secondly, it is a centre of excellence, not only for training the Army but also for research by the defence and technology industries; it is a centre of learning through its partnership with schools and universities; it has reached out to enthusiasts on a worldwide scale; and last but not least, it is undoubtedly the finest armoured vehicle museum in the world. Dorset should be very proud to have it as part of the county's culture and history.

tankmuseum.org

The centenary of the Dorset County Golf Union

Peter Fry reports

One hundred years of Dorset county golf were remembered at Came Down Golf Club on Wednesday 25 January 2023 with the unveiling of a commemorative stone alongside the first tee. Club presidents, club captains and other officials representing clubs from all over the county assembled at Came Down to celebrate, precisely one hundred years to the very day from the inauguration of the Dorset County Golf Union.

Back in 1923 the first committee meeting of a provisional 'Council' took place, representing seven Dorset golf clubs – Came Down, Dorset (Broadstone), Parkstone, Ferndown, West Dorset (Bridport), Ashley Wood (Blandford) and Isle of Purbeck. The meeting decided that it would be advantageous to form a county golf union to act as a central authority for determining all questions which may arise and to promote the welfare and the interests of the game in the county, and also to arrange with railway companies for increased travelling facilities for golfers. In addition, they decided to adopt the regulations of the Devon County Golf Union, suitably amended.

Within the inaugural year four more clubs had joined the original seven in the county union: Lyme Regis, Shaftesbury, Sherborne and Yeovil. An annual match was started between the professionals and the amateurs, as was a county foursomes competition for which clubs would enter one couple each.

It was decided to hold an annual championship meeting in which the winner of the 36-hole scratch competition would receive a gold medal and the runner-up a silver medal. Similarly a 36-hole handicap competition, with a handicap limit of 18, would be

Left to right: John Gordon (President, Dorset County Golf Union), Brian Hansford (President, Came Down Golf Club), Jeremy Tomlinson (CEO, England Golf)

run alongside the scratch event in which the respective winner and runner-up would also receive gold and silver medals. The entrance fee for both scratch and handicap events would be set at five shillings.

It was perhaps appropriate that the county union's first President, Captain Angus Hambro, won the first two scratch competitions at Broadstone and Came Down respectively. Hambro's skill as a player saw him play for England and later his administrative talents were sought as the Captain of the Royal & Ancient Golf Club of St Andrews (1928-1929) and as the President of the English Golf Union (1946), not to mention his role as an MP for South Dorset from 1910 to 1922 and North Dorset from 1937 to 1945.

Four county matches were quickly organised against the neighbouring counties of Devon, Hampshire, Somerset and Wiltshire. As a small county with fewer scratch handicaps than most, success has been limited over the succeeding years. However in 1991 Dorset won the Channel League for the first time in addition to victory in the South West Championship.

The team had cause for even greater celebration the following year when it won the English County Championship for the first time at Kings Norton Golf Club near Birmingham. The team started by defeating the reigning champions,, Middlesex, followed by victories over Yorkshire and Staffordshire. The players responsible for that historic success were Lee James of Broadstone, Roger Hearn and Steve Edgley of Parkstone, Peter McMullen and Martyn Thompson of Ferndown, Tony Lawrence of Sherborne and Michael Watson of Weymouth.

The centenary occasion was hosted by the President of the Dorset County Golf Union, John Gordon, who welcomed the guests headed by the CEO of England Golf, Jeremy Tomlinson. Gordon recounted aspects of the county's golf history, supported by golf historian Peter Fry. A highlight of this special occasion was a Q & A session with well-known Dorset golf champion Lee James, who reminisced about his British Amateur and Walker Cup victories and playing in the Open Championship and the Masters alongside golfing legends Jack Nicklaus and Tiger Woods.

The President of Came Down Golf Club, Brian Hansford, performed the official unveiling of the commemorative stone gifted to the Came Down club from the county union. Tomlinson then presented each individual Dorset golf club with a shield memento of the occasion.

www.dcgu.org.uk

www.camedowngolfclub.co.uk

The first bridge linking the old towns of Weymouth and Melcombe Regis was built in 1597, followed by a succession of replacements, including a rebuilding depicted here in the 1820s. It was a vital link to the south of Melcombe, but there was no access across the wide Backwater to the sprawling fields to the west of the town, hence the need for a Westham Bridge.

The first Westham Bridge

Stuart Morris tells of Weymouth's early attempts to make a crossing over the Backwater

For centuries the growing settlement of Melcombe Regis sat on a shingly peninsula, almost surrounded by water. To the east was the open sea, to the south was the historic harbour, and to the west was a vast area of tidal water known as the Backwater, stretching right up to Radipole village. Apart from a narrow neck of land on the north side, the only dry access to Melcombe was the Town Bridge, initially a timber structure erected in 1597. The lack of access to the west was not a major issue, as across the Backwater was still mostly farmland.

By the 1850s, however, the growing population of Melcombe Regis brought the desperate need for more burial space and with no room for this within the town, a new cemetery was laid out in the fields on the western side of the Backwater. The problem was that there was no path or road along that side of the Backwater, so the inhabitants had a long and tortuous trek to visit it. This prompted a group of worthies to promote a scheme for a bridge to cross the narrowest part of the Backwater.

Important schemes like this required Parliamentary approval, so The Backwater Bridge and Road Bill 1857 was launched to authorise the work. Not everyone was happy. There were many vested interests, including one councillor whose wife had £3000 of shares in the existing Town Bridge, the tolls income from which he feared would be worthless once the new bridge was open. Even the Town Council initially objected to the bill, fearing that the bridge would hinder development upstream.

Everyone would have to pay tolls to the Trustees to use the new bridge,

A detail of 'Pierse Arthur's Trigonometrical Map of Weymouth' of 1857. Arthur was a civil engineer and a highly competent architect. He designed the first Westham Bridge, clearly shown on his map. Also marked are the offices and timber yard of the contractor, Philip Dodson.

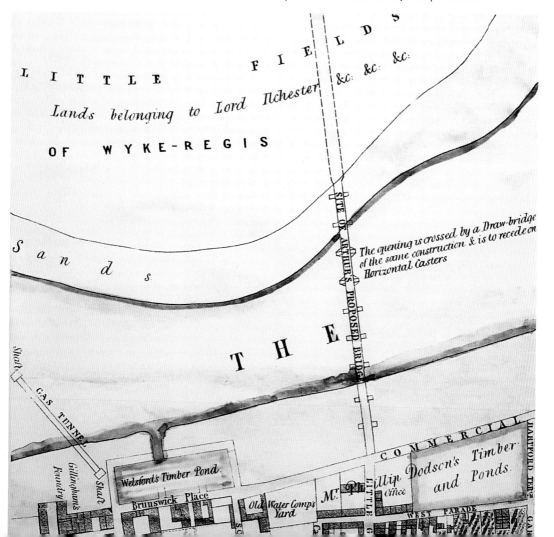

except for funerals and for access to any future docks. The bill stipulated that a swivel or opening bridge with a span of at least 50 feet must be included so that vessels could navigate to the upper reaches at all times, and there must be a minimum clearance of six feet from water to deck at all states of the tide. Everything had to be approved by the Admiralty, as these were tidal waters.

Pierse Arthur, a prominent civil engineer and architect, was commissioned to produce the design for the bridge. With his surveyors, he made a detailed plan of the entire Melcombe Regis area in 1856. Prominently marked on his map was his proposed bridge. He worked closely with Philip Dodson, a prolific and wealthy builder, developer and timber merchant, who was Borough Mayor three times in the 1850s. (Dodson had acquired a large plot of vacant land at the Narrows, towards the north end of the sea front, where in 1855-57 he built a magnificent hotel, designed by Pierse Arthur, and named it after his friend, William Burdon, proprietor of the gas works. The Burdon Hotel was much later renamed the Hotel Prince Regent.)

Philip Dodson's other achievements were of mind-blowing scale. With his army of skilled tradesmen and workers, he constructed a pioneering long and wide brick tunnel for a gas pipe under the bed of the Backwater, and his firm constructed the great Bincombe Tunnel at Ridgeway on the Dorchester to Weymouth railway line as well as the original clifftop convict prison at Portland. His crowning glory was St John's church, whose tall spire has dominated the Weymouth skyline since 1854.

Against all that the new timber bridge must have been seen as a doddle, but it was to prove his downfall.

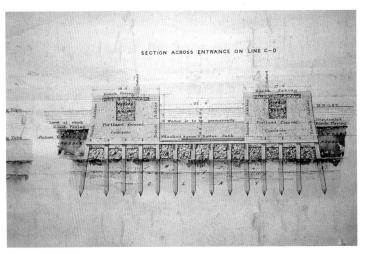

The upper reaches of the Backwater were increasingly plagued with stinking mudbanks when the tide went out. Engineer Sir John Coode (of Portland Breakwater fame) was engaged to come up with a solution. In 1872 he designed a robust weir downstream of the bridge to retain the water level, with a gated opening (seen here) to permit the passage of barges and boats. Unfortunately, that did not resolve all the problems.

Pierse Arthur's 250-yard-long timber bridge from the Melcombe Regis town side, built by Philip Dodson in 1859-60, opened the way for vast building development on the Westham fields. The top of Coode's weir is just visible (foreground), retaining the water at high tide.

Dodson started the construction of the bridge in July 1859 and progress was rapid. Heavy timber piles were driven into the river bed, and a pile-driving machine was floated into position to drive supports for the central gate piers. Stone piers were erected at each end of the 40-foot-wide roadway. Located some 200 metres downstream of the position of the modern Swannery Bridge, the new link to the west side offered immense prospects. It connected Little George Street (now Westham Road) via a new road (now Abbotsbury Road) through the fields to the turnpike road to Chickerell. Reports said: 'Weymouth will have a chance of extending itself, in the shape of suburban villas, arising like fairy palaces under the magic manipulations of the master mason.' Whether the vast housing developments that followed, across the fields of Westham, met that vision is not clear, but there aren't many fairy palaces in evidence!

The 250-yard timber bridge was almost complete by May 1860 when one of the supports nearly collapsed and had to be propped up with blocks. That did not augur well for the bridge, which became dogged by more and more issues. The problems must have weighed heavily on Philip Dodson, for in July 1860 he killed himself by taking cyanide 'while under the influence of temporary insanity', as the inquest said. His cortege took the long way around to the cemetery, pointedly avoiding passing over the bridge he had just built. Sadly, Dodson's simple gravestone in the Melcombe cemetery tells nothing of his great achievements.

Until additional supports were installed, the bridge structure was not strong enough to support the weight of carriages, so only pedestrians could use it. Barges and boats found navigating past the bridge a challenge, as the tidal

Looking westward towards the yet-to-be-developed Westham. The construction of the timber bridge across the muddy tidal Backwater proved a formidable challenge for builder Dodson. By the 1880s the bridge had deteriorated to a dangerous state, but 'Unsafe Bridge' notices at each end were ignored, as the link was now vital for the growing population of residents.

currents caused them to crash into the piles. Soon after, the much more substantial timber viaduct for the Portland Railway was constructed just upstream.

The new Westham Bridge did nothing to control the flow of water, which was becoming increasingly contaminated with the town's smelly sewage, discharged from both sides into the Backwater. A solution was desperately needed, so in 1871 the famous John Coode, engineer of the great Portland Breakwaters, was commissioned to produce a scheme to deal with it. Detailed sections and borings were taken. In addition to new sewers and outfalls, Coode recommended that a masonry dam or weir be constructed just below the bridge to ensure that upstream, water covered the stinking mud banks at all tides. The dam was to have an 18-foot opening in the centre to permit the passage of barges and boats. A gate was included to retain the water at the required level. Coode's dam had a core of clay and sheet piling, surmounted with shaped Portland roach stone paving. Two substantial masonry piers flanked the central gap. A timber gangway from the Melcombe side gave access to the single-leaf tide gate.

The dam was constructed by contractor Joseph Phillips in 1872, but within two years two large holes appeared in the bed above and below the dam, and further urgent repairs were carried out in 1884. Despite modifications, the dam did not cure all the problems: 'The stink coming from the Backwater is very objectionable, arising from the exposure of the sewage to sun and heat on the dry mud banks, decaying seaweed and the constant irritation of the sewage by the rush of water over the dam.' The banks were overrun with rats, which in July 1886 reportedly killed 50 young cygnets. Residents had to live with the stench until well into the 20th century. Nevertheless, Coode's dam remained almost intact until being demolished for the new inner harbour marina in 1995.

The halfpenny tolls were abolished when the bridge was declared a County Bridge in 1879, but the County still argued that the Borough should pay to repair it. The bridge was now in such a dangerous state that users' lives were in peril. The Borough Surveyor declared in May 1880 that it was unsafe even for existing traffic. Notices were posted at each end stating 'Unsafe Bridge', but these were ignored.

The road bridge needed frequent repairs and modifications, while the timbers inevitably continued to rot. In 1882 the bridge had to be closed for major repairs. Piles and decking were replaced and the opening section was replaced by a fixed deck, finally enabling full use by carts and light carriages. The new residents of sprawling Westham suburb now petitioned for a proper footpath along the bridge, which was eventually created in 1891. However, two years later a further petition complained of the danger of children falling through the open gaps in the recently constructed footway.

Despite everything, the bridge link remained a busy lifeline. A count on one day in 1884 showed that the bridge was crossed by 570 vehicles, 140 horses, 125 cattle and 537 pedestrians, all struggling to pass over the failing deck. In 1914 Dorset passed responsibility back to the Borough Council. A replacement bridge of stone was planned, but of course everything stopped for the Great War.

The final word on this infamous first Westham Bridge must

This map shows the rapidly developing Westham area in the 1890s. Note the Backwater Bridge, John Coode's weir, the railway viaduct of 1864, and the Melcombe Regis Burial Ground, where bridge contractor Philip Dodson was laid to rest in 1860.

go to Kathleen Betts, a girl of Weymouth Secondary School (later the Grammar School), which had been built on the Westham side in 1913. In 1919 she wrote this little piece which she called 'Now, Westham Bridge':

> *Now, Westham Bridge is in a state of ruin, and one day, with all its passengers, will collapse and fall into the Backwater.*
>
> *Now, the town councillors converse in their chamber, of repairs; 'Shall the bridge be repaired or not?' 'What will the cost be?*
>
> *Now, the ratepayers dread to see the result of the last meeting. They need not worry. It has not been carried out for twenty years and is not likely to be for another twenty.*
>
> *Now, the rain comes beating into the faces of the poor pedestrians and all those who cannot ride in closed vehicles.*
>
> *Now, the wind rushes up the skirts of the poor school-girls who tramp across the rickety bridge four times a day.*
>
> *Now, one of the Corinthians studies her 'Latin' when splash! Down fall her homework books into the water. She wonders what will happen when she goes to see the powers that-be, and her books have to be replaced!*
>
> *Now, the keeper goes on his daily round to feed the swans, which have returned to their island home.*
>
> *Now, the 'Portland Express' crawls past the end of the bridge, making the framework shake, while the school-girl shakes in her shoes because the gates are shut and it is five minutes to nine.*
>
> *Now, the pupils of W.S.S. cross the bridge two abreast according to rule 1.*
>
> *Now, the bridge is so shaky that it can only support two tons. Now a motor lorry comes along – load three tons. What is it to do? What! No police about? That's good! Chance it? Yes! Away it spins over the bridge, making it rattle. This will happen once too often, sad to say.*
>
> *Now, the weary Westhamers return from town and get blown away, owing to the lack of corrugated iron at the sides.*
>
> *Now, the longing eyes of a W.S.S. pupil scan the sheet of water which she hopes will be filled in for a hockey pitch – one day. Echo says, 'One day!'*

The end of the old bridge was nigh, though, and in 1919, the council adopted a scheme to build a new solid embankment bridge, engineered to the latest revolutionary principles.

Through to the main line

Andrew P M Wright explains how the Swanage Railway achieved the dream of running regular passenger trains to Wareham again after more than 50 years

When teenager Peter Frost rode on the last British Rail train from Swanage to Wareham on the cold night of Saturday 1 January 1972, he never imagined that 51 years later he would be the conductor driver of the first train into Wareham using the Swanage Railway's restored 1950s diesel unit.

With his parents running the popular Greyhound pub below the dramatic ruins of Corfe Castle during the 1960s and 1970s, Peter

The last day of British Rail trains between Swanage and Wareham with a 1950s diesel train from Wareham waiting at Corfe Castle station on Saturday 1 January 1972. The track through here was ripped up for scrap in August 1972, with a bypass planned for the railway trackbed through Corfe Castle until 1986.

watched the ten-mile branch line from Wareham to Swanage run down for more than five years before controversial closure, after which the fourteen-year-old witnessed seven miles of track being ripped up for scrap in just seven weeks during the summer of 1972. From that sad summer, a determined Peter – now a retired engineer living in Swanage who has been a Swanage Railway volunteer steam and diesel train driver since the late 1970s – resolved to help re-build the branch line; he was one of the first volunteers to start restoring a boarded up and near-derelict Swanage station in February 1976.

Re-building the Swanage Railway has been a slow process as the track was re-laid yard by yard and by hand initially. The first new station in Dorset for more than 50 years was built at Harman's Cross, three miles from Swanage, in 1988. The first public trains ran into the station during March 1989, when it was officially opened by Gordon Pettitt, the General Manager of British Rail's

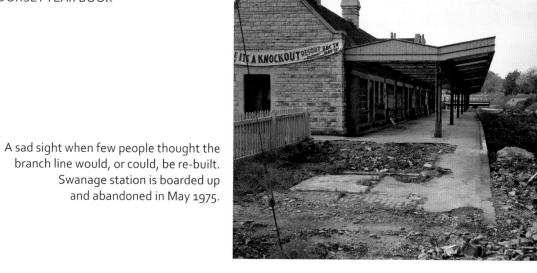

A sad sight when few people thought the branch line would, or could, be re-built. Swanage station is boarded up and abandoned in May 1975.

Southern Region – the region that had controversially closed the Swanage line 17 years earlier.

Swanage Railway volunteers continued to re-lay the track two miles further on to Corfe Castle, whose overgrown and boarded up Victorian station was reached during the summer of 1990. Restoration work started at the station, and meanwhile the track was re-laid half a mile further on to Norden, where a station was built with Purbeck District Council creating a large car park next to the new station. The first steam trains ran along the 5½ miles of line between Swanage, Corfe Castle and Norden in August 1995, after which a period of consolidation followed for the heritage line.

After the Swanage branch closed to passenger trains in January 1972, the three miles of line from Worgret Junction – west of Wareham on the main London to Weymouth line – to Furzebrook was used for the export of Purbeck ball clay. With the development of oil extraction at Wytch Farm, north of Corfe Castle, a rail export terminal was opened at Furzebrook in 1979 and oil and gas were taken out by train from there until 2005, when a pipeline was built for that purpose and the line from Worgret Junction was mothballed by Network Rail.

In the summer of 1999, the Swanage Railway started a push to clear undergrowth from the final mile-long section of abandoned trackbed and to re-lay the track from Norden to Motala, half a mile east of Furzebrook, which was the end of the national railway network and where the line was blocked. In January 2002, 30 years to the day after the branch line was closed by British Rail, the Swanage Railway's re-laid tracks reached the start of the national railway network at Motala and five years later, the Swanage Railway's tracks were connected to those of Network Rail at Motala. That historic connection to the national railway system enabled diesel- and steam-hauled excursion trains to run from London to Corfe Castle and Swanage during April and May 2009, for the first time since 1972 and 1967 respectively.

The future of the Swanage Railway's connection to the national system was ensured in 2012 thanks to the upgrading of Worgret Junction with new signalling and tracks by Network Rail. Thanks to the Purbeck Community Rail Partnership – of which the Swanage Railway and Network Rail are members – the vital future-proofing work was paid for by a £3.2 million grant from Purbeck District Council, funded by a transport improvement tax on developers building new housing in the Purbeck area.

In 2014, ownership of three miles of mothballed line from ¼ mile south of Worgret Junction to Motala was transferred in 2014 from Network Rail to Dorset County Council, which leased the track to the Swanage Railway. A new and innovative signalling system was devised to link the Swanage Railway with Network Rail's upgraded main line signalling system between Poole, Wareham and Wool. Swanage Railway signalling equipment was installed on the platform at Wareham station and when trains run from the Swanage Railway onto the national railway system – and vice versa – the signalman at Corfe Castle station's Victorian-style signal box liaises with the Network Rail signalling centre at Basingstoke in Hampshire.

The grant money also went towards the Swanage Railway's overhaul and upgrade of two former British Railways 1950s heritage diesel multiple unit trains – one composed of three carriages and the other of one carriage – so they could run on the main line into Wareham station. Specialist contractors fitted the same

Below left: Network Rail upgrades the track and signalling at Worgret Junction – where Swanage Railway trains bound for Wareham run onto the main London to Weymouth line – during December 2012. Below right: Swanage Railway staff and volunteers lay new track on the former Network Rail line at Furzebrook, between Corfe Castle and Worgret Junction, during 2015.

Approaching Worgret Junction and the start of the mile-long journey along the main line into Wareham station, a Swanage Railway 1950s heritage diesel multiple unit crosses the River Frome water meadows on Tuesday 4 April 2023. In the distance are Creech Barrow and the Purbeck Hills.

technical, signalling and safety equipment in the trains that is installed on all trains running on the national railway network.

During the summer of 2017, the Swanage Railway operated a 60-day trial train service to Wareham, using hired-in diesel locomotives and carriages operated and staffed by West Coast Railways. It had been hoped to operate a second trial during 2018, but this was delayed. Then the Covid pandemic hit, and its practical and economic effects meant that the second trial was postponed until 2023. Thus it was on Tuesday 4 April 2023 that the Swanage Railway's own heritage diesel trains started a 90-day trial train service to Wareham, and in the cab of the train on that first historic day was conductor driver Peter Frost. A delighted Peter recalled that special and poignant occasion: 'I certainly felt the hand of history on my shoulder. It was a great moment when our 1950s heritage diesel train ran into Wareham for the first time and then departed ten minutes later bound for Corfe Castle and Swanage – something that several generations of dedicated and determined Swanage Railway volunteers have worked towards since 1972.'

An historic day and turning back the clock to before 1972. The first Swanage Railway 1950s heritage diesel multiple unit train runs into Wareham from Corfe Castle on Tuesday 4 April 2023, with conductor driver Peter Frost in the cab.

With four trains a day operating between Wareham, Corfe Castle and Swanage on Saturdays, Tuesdays, Wednesdays and Thursdays, the last day of the trial train service was on Saturday 9 September 2023. Tickets for the Swanage Railway's trial Wareham service were available from main line train operating company South Western Railway, so its passengers could purchase add-on tickets for Corfe Castle and Swanage to their main line tickets. It was the first time in 51 years that such a main line ticket facility for train travel to Swanage had been possible.

Gavin Johns, the volunteer chairman of the Swanage Railway Trust, which manages the volunteer-run heritage line, said: 'Our trial train service to Wareham was the result of working in partnership with the Government's Coastal Communities Fund, the Department of Transport, the former Purbeck District Council, Dorset Council, British Petroleum, Perenco, Network Rail and South Western Railway. I would like to thank our valued stakeholders for their far-sighted investment of £5.5 million to re-connect Swanage and Corfe

Conductor driver Peter Frost uses the Swanage Railway signalling equipment on Wareham station before the 1950s heritage diesel multiple unit train returns to Corfe Castle and Swanage on its inaugural scheduled passenger run

Castle with the main line at Wareham, which included £1.8 million from the Government's Coastal Communities Fund,' added Gavin, who is also a volunteer Swanage Railway signalman.

The conductor guard on the first day of the Swanage Railway's Wareham heritage diesel train service in April was volunteer guard and signalman Trevor Parsons, who is chairman of the Swanage Railway Company – which runs the heritage trains – and also a director of the Swanage Railway Trust. Trevor

The Swanage Railway's 1950s heritage diesel multiple unit train at Wareham station before it departs for Corfe Castle and Swanage

explained: 'I would like to thank our stakeholders for their help and patience over many years with a complicated and historic project that has been as ambitious as it has been challenging. Seeing happy passengers on our Wareham trains has made all the hard work worthwhile.' Purbeck Community Rail Partnership chairman, Councillor Mike Whitwam, said: 'The Swanage Railway's trial train service to the main line at Wareham marked an important opportunity to return to a fully functioning and sustainable rail service meeting the needs of local communities, visitors and businesses. It enabled Isle of Purbeck residents to travel anywhere possible by rail, leaving their cars at home and taking traffic off the congested A351 road,' added Mike, who is also a Swanage Railway Trust trustee and Swanage town councillor.

Anyone interested in volunteering should contact the Swanage Railway volunteer recruitment and retention office on 01929 475212 or email iwanttovolunteer@ swanagerailway.co.uk. More details about volunteering opportunities can be found at swanagerailwaytrust.org/volunteering.

Lewesdon Hill

The ancient woods on Lewesdon Hill
Are paradise to me,
For under summer skies I find
Profound serenity.

But does the beauty draw me here
To these enchanted glades?
Or does some siren spirit haunt
The woods as twilight fades?

The beauty here is manifest:
The restless sighing trees,
The view across the sunken vale
Of distant sparkling seas,

The scent of woodbine, wild briar rose
And fresh unsullied dawn,
The glory of the dappled light
That hides the sleeping fawn.

But spirits too seem still to drift
About this sacred place,
Of Marshwood men who tilled the soil
But left no earthly trace.

And when my spirit shall be free
To wander like the breeze,
I think that it will settle too
Like mist about these trees.

David Bushrod

Beaminster Grammar School, the Buglers and the Hardy Players

Digby Barker describes the connection

M y connection with Dorset began when, as a 10-year-old, I moved to Melbury Abbas. In 1959 I was sent off as a boarder to the then Beaminster & Netherbury Grammar School (BNGS), where I remained until leaving for university in 1966. I have maintained many friendships from that period through frequent visits to the county, particularly to Beaminster in connection with reunions of the school's Old Boys & Old Girls Association (OBOGA), and to Weymouth where my sister and family live.

In organising a recent celebration of the centenary of the founding of the OBOGA, I became aware of a connection, albeit slight, between the association

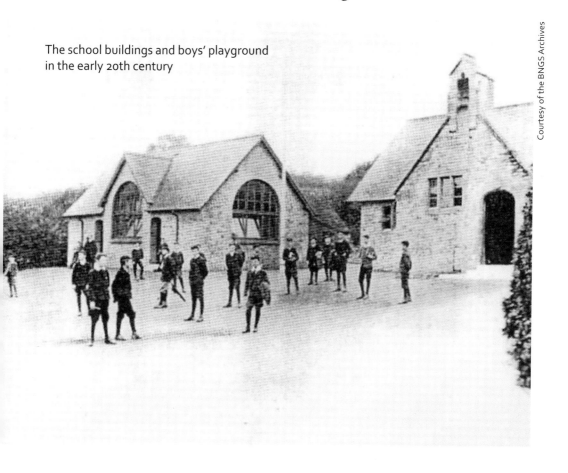

The school buildings and boys' playground
in the early 20th century

Courtesy of the BNGS Archives

and the Hardy Players. The connection was new to me and of particular interest because I had just finished reading John Travell's article in the *Dorset Year Book* for 2017, 'Thomas Hardy and the Hardy Players'. As the background to this connection requires a summary of the school's history, this also complements the previous *Year Book* articles on Beaminster, the most recent being Douglas Beazer's 'An insight into Beaminster', which appears in the 2022 edition.

Beaminster & Netherbury Grammar School (BNGS) was formally opened in 1881 on the amalgamation of Beaminster's Tucker School (which had been established in 1703 through a bequest by Mrs Francis Tucker of Mapperton) with the grammar school from the nearby village of Netherbury. According to Richard Hine's 1914 *History of Beaminster*, Netherbury Grammar School had been founded in 1564 – an auspicious year as it also saw the birth of both Shakespeare and Galileo! On the 1881 amalgamation, the governors

Courtesy of the BNGS Archives

Arthur 'Weeds' Graveson working in the school's agriculture plot had difficulty finding a suitable site for the new school and there was residual opposition in Netherbury over the loss of its grammar school, so it was 1897 before a permanent location was established on the site of the Old Potteries in Hogshill Street.

By the early 20th century, BNGS was already regarded as a centre of excellence for agriculture, which was 'the mainstay of local industry', to quote Douglas Beazer's article about Beaminster in the *Dorset Year Book* for 2022. The County Council provided one of its agriculture inspectors to assist with the subject's teaching, and agriculture scholarships were awarded. This reputation was enhanced from 1919 by the efforts and enthusiasm of a well-loved, long-serving biology and agriculture teacher, Mr Arthur Graveson – known affectionately as 'Weeds' – who also established a Field Club at the school to encourage the identification of botanical species in the area. With the help of the pupils he inspired, he was able to compile a catalogue of the flora of West Dorset, and the Botanical Society of Britain and Ireland has some 80 plants attributed to him in its herbaria.

In January 1963, BNGS was incorporated, along with Beaminster boys' secondary school and girls over 11 from the local girls' school, into a new, purpose-built comprehensive school (the 'New School') in the Newtown area. Boy boarders continued to live on the site of the old grammar school and girl boarders at 'Woodlands' – which had been acquired as a girls' boarding house in 1953 and was safely at the other end of town! – until the properties were sold off in the mid-1990s.

The grammar school's Old Boys & Old Girls Association (OBOGA) was formed in 1923 with Mr Graveson as its founding treasurer. Thereafter the association organised or facilitated reunions of former pupils and staff and although it made efforts to encourage those leaving the New School to join, this met with limited success. Consequently, by 2017 it was clear that the association would have to be formally wound up as the ageing membership found it increasingly difficult to meet the physical demands of organising such gatherings. So there were to be no more large-scale reunions, but individual year groups continue to meet for walks and other activities, with the last OBOGA secretary, Lesley Rundle, continuing to facilitate contact. Her 2011 *BNGS Years Book*, put together as a pictorial record incorporating former pupils' photos and reminiscences, is one of two that have been published by the association, the other being her 2015 *BNGS Teachers Book*. These complement

former pupil Derek Woodland's *A History of the Beaminster and Netherbury Grammar School,* which he published in 2005 and on which I have drawn in outlining the above history.

Fortunately, some ex-pupils remembered that 26 July 2023 marked the centenary of the association's formation and organised a celebratory afternoon tea. The first boys' secretary of OBOGA had been Ernest Bugler, and a guest at the tea was Mike Toms, his grandson. Ernest married his cousin, Gertrude Bugler (so confusingly, both her married and her maiden names were Bugler) and the name reminded me of John Travell's article on the Hardy Players in the *Dorset Year Book* for 2017 because Gertrude Bugler was the Hardy Players' leading lady in a number of their productions. Mike's mother, Diana Toms (née Bugler), attended BNGS, became the school's domestic science teacher for many years beyond the creation of the New School, and was a regular attender at OBOGA reunions. At the tea, Mike was able to quote his grandmother, Gertrude, in scotching the rumours that Hardy had been infatuated with her. Florence Hardy, the poet's second wife, was nevertheless suspicious and paid what in his article John Travell called an 'extraordinarily emotional' visit to Gertrude to warn her off her planned London appearance in *Tess of the d'Urbervilles.*

Courtesy of the BNGS Archives

Left: Gertrude Bugler in a publicity shot for a Hardy Players production

Above: Gertrude's daughter, Diana, as a pupil at Beaminster Grammar School and after retirement as the school's domestic science teacher

St Mary's, East Lulworth

Jeremy Archer on the history of the first free-standing Catholic church to be completed in England after the Reformation in 1538

That St Mary's, East Lulworth, was built in the first place is all the more surprising when one bears in mind the Weld family's links with Maria Anne Smythe, known to history simply as Mrs Fitzherbert. Her first husband was Edward Weld of Lulworth, a wealthy widower sixteen years her senior. Sadly, Edward died intestate just three months later following a fall from a horse, so his younger brother, Thomas, inherited the Lulworth Estate, leaving Maria in desperate financial straits. In 1778 she married Thomas Fitzherbert of Swynnerton, Staffordshire, who was a decade older than her. He died in 1781 but left her an annuity of £1000 – the equivalent of almost £150,000 in today's terms – together with a town house in London's Mayfair.

Thus launched into society under favourable circumstances, Maria soon attracted the attention of George, Prince of Wales, later King George IV. Following an ardent, single-minded pursuit, George, who was six years younger than Maria, persuaded her to marry him, which she did at her house in Park Street in 1785. Without the prior approval of King George III and the Privy

Council, the ceremony was in direct contravention of the Royal Marriages Act 1772 and was therefore invalid. Even had approval been given, Maria's Catholicism would have ensured George's removal from the line of succession, under the provisions of the Bill of Rights and the Act of Settlement 1701.

Thomas Weld, Maria's former brother-in-law, not unnaturally wished to have a place where he and his Roman Catholic family could worship in the traditional manner instead of using the room on the first floor of Lulworth Castle which was later to become their dining room. He therefore instructed John Tasker to design a private chapel in the park. The key fact was that it was free-standing. A decade earlier, at New Wardour Castle in Wiltshire, Henry, eighth Baron Arundell of Wardour, had instructed James Paine to include a chapel in the west wing in as unobtrusive a way as possible. The chapel at Wardour was the first new Catholic chapel, open for public worship, to be built since the Reformation and Evelyn Waugh is thought to have used it as the model for the chapel at Brideshead. But it was not free-standing.

Because of his son's pursuit of Maria Fitzherbert and because of her history, King George III might have been ill-disposed towards the Welds, but the family story is that the King gave his consent, saying words to the effect of 'Build a family mausoleum and you can furnish the inside as a Catholic chapel if you wish.'

Great attention and expense was lavished on the 'Great Chapel', construction of which began in the late autumn of 1785, when Bindon stone was ordered for the plinth and Portland stone for the building itself. In order to cover his tracks, Thomas issued instructions that the coffins of his ancestors should be transferred from the vault in the parish church to the new building, thus lending credibility to his insistence that it was indeed a mausoleum and silencing any doubters. On 30 December 1786, the Jesuit Father John Thorpe described in a letter written in Rome the exquisite craftsmanship of Giacomo Quarenghi's altar, the crucifix and the six gilt-bronze candlesticks, noting that the Pope 'was pleased to commend and admire them'. After being shipped from Italy, the altar was set up in February 1787. The organ, made by Richard Seede of Bristol in 1785, was originally intended to be installed in the castle, in which case it would certainly have been destroyed in the devastating fire of 1929. Instead, it now fits very snugly on one of the first-floor galleries, below

St Mary's from the south

a domed transept ceiling, having been restored by the Baltimore-born organ builder, William Drake, in 1986.

There is no contemporary documentary proof for the family story of Royal assent, but there is strong evidence that the Weld family was on good terms with the Royal family: King George III first visited Weymouth for the sake of his health in the summer of 1789, finding time to pay his first visit to Lulworth Castle. King George III and Queen Charlotte visited Lulworth on four occasions in all, in successive years.

On 7 August 1789, Thomas Weld wrote to Lord Arundell: 'We have at length got this Royal Visit to the castle over.... I conducted them to the rooms below, the eating parlour, Chapel, breakfast room etc. From thence we went round the pleasure ground and arrived at the principal entrance of the Great Chapel. The King asked me two or three times what building that was and I told him and just before we got to it he asked again and then I asked if his Majesty would choose to see the inside. He said yes; accordingly the doors were flung open.... I am very glad this business is over. I hope it will answer

Top of page: The south front with Tuscan columns, entablature and niches housing carved urns

Left : The sanctuary after the Victorian 'restoration'

Opposite: The nave, looking towards the altar

The organ and altar from the southern gallery

the purpose I had solely in view; I think the King's seeing the Chapel in that publick manner might be a kind of sanction to it.' Although the King had been unwell for some time, Thomas's letter betrays a certain nervousness and gives no indication of prior Royal agreement to his construction project. Perhaps he feared that, without 'planning permission', he might be told to tear his new chapel down!

The first specific mention of Royal approval in the family archives does not emerge until almost a century later, in a letter written by Charles Weld of Chideock in 1879. Whatever the truth of the story, the chapel certainly bears a far greater resemblance to a jewel-like Palladian country villa than it does to a Roman Catholic chapel.

St Mary's swiftly gained acceptance and renown. John Carroll, the first Roman Catholic bishop, and then archbishop, in the United States and founder of Georgetown University, was ordained a bishop in St Mary's by Bishop Charles Walmesley on 15 August 1790, the Feast of the Assumption. The following week, in a joint ceremony, the Right Reverend John Douglass was consecrated Vicar Apostolic of the London District while the Right Reverend William Gibson was consecrated Vicar Apostolic of the Northern District. The following year, the Roman Catholic Relief Act 1791 was passed; among other things, Catholics were now permitted the exercise of their religion. The long title reads: 'An act to relieve, upon conditions, and under restrictions, the persons therein described, from certain penalties and disabilities to which papists, or persons professing the popish religion, are by law subject.'

During the 1860s, the prevailing fashion decreed that the plain Georgian building should be given a makeover in the Byzantine style. J R Hansom (who designed the hansom cab) was awarded the contract, with the result that the interior was thoroughly 'Victorianised'. The exterior was not exempt from this treatment and the original sixteen-pane, Georgian windows were replaced by double-lancet, round-headed windows with leaded diamond panes and stained-glass roundels. What had been an impressively light interior now resembled the supposed mausoleum on the basis of which construction had been approved in the first place. Just in case that was not enough, the walls, ceilings, spandrels and pendentives (which allow a dome to be placed over a square or rectangular space) were also painted, while inscriptions were added, much sculpture introduced and religious canvases placed on the walls. To modern eyes, it would have appeared rather oppressive.

'Assumption of the Blessed Virgin Mary'
by Sarah Jansen, 1987

Help was at hand. In 1953, the highly respected architect, writer and musician, Harry Stuart Goodhart-Rendel, was entrusted with the task of returning St Mary's to something closer to Thomas Weld's vision. The fenestration was returned to the original designs, with glazing bars; the window glass was replaced; Weld family funerary lozenges were hung on the newly whitewashed walls; the woodwork was refreshed; much gilding was introduced; oval classical scenes in subdued colours were painted on the pendentives and a satisfyingly stripped-down look achieved. The crowning glory is the painting of the domed ceiling, which depicts the Assumption of the Blessed Virgin Mary. Designed by Sarah Jansen in 1983, the work was completed in time for the Chapel's bicentenary in 1987.

lulworth.com

'He was the last man I should have ever thought capable of standing the strain of that sort of thing.'

Brian Bates tells the inspiring story of Harold Swain

The comment that forms the title of this article appeared in a staff newsletter written by Mr Edwards, partner in the firm of Dorchester accountants Edwards and Edwards, in March 1943. The person referred to was one of his employees, 22-year-old Harold Swain.

I first met Harold Swain some fifty years later at a Bayeux Society dinner. During the course of the meal, I overheard him telling another diner that he had been in Bomber Command during World War 2. This aroused my curiosity, so later in the evening I asked him about his experiences and learnt his remarkable story.

Harold was born in 1921 at Frome Whitfield, just outside Dorchester. His parents moved into the town, where the family lived at 46 The Grove, and Harold went to the nearby West Fordington School. He then attended Dorchester Boys School in Colliton Street, where he excelled in mathematics. Outside the classroom he was a keen sportsman and a regular member of the Boys' Brigade.

Harold was aged 19 on the outbreak of World War 2 and working as a clerk/typist at Edwards and Edwards. Also working in the office was a young lady named Madge, who later became his wife. The war had been going on for a year when he and his mates decided that it was time they did their bit and applied for admission into the Royal Air Force Volunteer Reserve. Harold told me that they were just a bunch of lads looking for adventure.

His application obviously impressed and he began the recruitment process to fulfil his wish to be a pilot. The Air Candidates Selection Board decided that he was eligible to become a flyer, but any thoughts he had of taking to the air straightaway were thwarted when he was given two choices. Either he could defer his entry for six months or he could join an ack-ack battery for six months before he entered the RAF. He chose the former option, not wanting to risk deafness. Six months later, Harold was before another board which tested, among other things, whether he could reach an aircraft's rudder control with his feet – he was only 5' 2" tall. The test was passed and Harold's ambition to become a pilot was nearer, only to be dashed when the selection board recommended the job of radio operator/gunner. Disappointed, he accepted.

Essential to the role of wireless operator was being able to send and receive morse code messages, which Harold found easy as he had learned morse to a proficient standard in the Boys' Brigade. Passing out as an 'A' student after seven months at RAF Yatesbury Signals School, where he learned about all aspects of radio equipment and wireless communication, he was, much to his surprise, given the rank of sergeant although he had not yet flown. It was now time for gunnery training, at which Harold declared that he was useless; he was thankful that he never had to shoot in anger throughout the war.

Next, the newly qualified radio operator was sent to No.14 Operational Training Unit at Cottesmore in West Sussex, just south of Gatwick Airport. It was here that the aircrews were formed. An airman was not assigned to a crew; instead, they were encouraged to form groups among themselves. Harold's flying logbook shows that he took his first flight on 12 October 1942, in a Wellington bomber. During this time he flew with various pilots, but on 25 October, his pilot was an American sergeant from Connecticut named Jerome Zee, who had not waited for America to join the war but enlisted in the Royal Canadian Air Force in 1940. The two men jelled and a crew was soon formed, consisting of two Americans, a New Zealander and five Englishmen. In the months ahead they would become a team, each relying on the others for his life.

While they were forming and training at Cottesmore, the crews were

The young airman and Madge were married in December 1942

Harold and his crew outside their Stirling, W7259. Behind, left to right: Eric Lewin, navigator; Fred Darlington, gunner; Harold; David Johnson, engineer. Kneeling: Bill Bradford, bomb aimer; Jerry Zee, pilot; Morton Hindmarsh, gunner.

probably unaware that they were being closely observed for a very particular reason: the best of them were to be invited to join the newly established Pathfinders.

The Pathfinder force was created to improve Bomber Command's lamentable efforts at accurate bombing. Their role on a raid was to be the first aircraft over the target and to mark it by dropping different-coloured flares. The second wave of bombers were then directed by a master bomber to drop their bombs on the area indicated. A Pathfinder crew's job was particularly hazardous. The pilot had to make his approach to the target at a steady speed and a flat altitude, something the German gunners on the ground knew only too well, and it was then that they were most likely to bring a plane down. The commanding officer of the Pathfinder squadrons was an Australian, Group Captain Donald Bennett, who expected the highest standards from his crews; they were continually monitored and if they were below par, they were sent back to a conventional squadron.

Harold joined 7 Squadron Pathfinder Force at RAF Oakington, near Cambridge, in March 1943, and immediately his chances of finishing the war considerably decreased. Had he joined one of the other bomber squadrons, he would have been required to carry out 30 operations before completing a tour, but Bennett demanded that his crews complete 45. Added to this, the general statistics on survival in Bomber Command make grim reading: at the time Harold undertook his first operation, only one in six crews was expected to

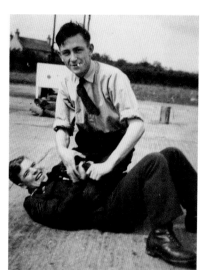

Right: Harold skylarking with rear gunner Morton Hindmarsh

Below, left to right: Flight Sergeant Porteus, DFM and bar; Warrant Officer Fagan; Harold; Pilot Officer Wilson, DSO, DFC, DFM. Harold flew with them on a Berlin raid on 2 December 1943. Wilson and Porteus were both killed in 1944 and Fagan became a prisoner of war.

finish a tour. One airman described going on a bombing operation as like going over the top on the first day at the battle of the Somme. The difference was that a Pathfinder had to do it 45 times with little respite in between.

Harold's first operation was to St Nazaire in France, in a Stirling bomber piloted by Jerry Zee. The raid was uneventful, although the operation was not very successful: part of the target was the German submarine pens, covered with huge concrete roofs which easily withstood the bombs.

In the spring of 1943, the battle of the Ruhr, aimed at Germany's industrial heartland, began. On the evening of 2 / 3 March, Zee piloted his crew on the first operation of the battle. The target was Essen and the raid consisted of 442 bombers. Ahead of them were five Mosquito aircraft that dropped marker flares fifteen miles from the target, where the main force was to begin its run-in. Then the 22 Pathfinders went ahead and dropped yellow flares over the target and, after taking photographs, headed for home. Harold's plane returned to Oakington safely, with a few flak splinters, but fourteen other crews were not so lucky.

On the night of 14/15 April 1943, Harold and his crew were joined by 461 other bombers making their way to the Kent coast, then across northern France, on to Luxemburg and so to their target for tonight, Stuttgart. The Pathfinders encountered fierce flak over the city, which made marking difficult, and the main force's bombing was not accurate. The duration of this raid was nearly seven hours in pitch darkness. A long flight was always difficult, particularly the trip home. By this time the German night fighters had been scrambled and the bomber crews were tired. Jerry Zee's two gunners had been staring into the black sky for hours on end when suddenly a Junkers 88 came out of the darkness, guns blazing. The gunners managed to see off the German plane, but not before it had torn several holes in the bomber's fuselage.

During the round journey, Harold was continually checking inter-plane radio frequencies and receiving messages from base. He also had the very important job of looking after the homing pigeon that had to be released in the event of a ditching. It was important that he knew the exact location of the plane at any one time in case of such an event; should the crew need to bail out, he would be the last to leave, having given the most up-to-date position.

The fierce flak experienced over Stuttgart and attacking fighters were not the only things that Harold and his crew had to contend with. Along with the occasional engine failure there was extreme weather. This was illustrated during an operation to Hamburg on the night of 2/3 August 1943. On the night in question Zee left Oakington, easing his Lancaster into an overcast and blustery sky. (Harold had a new job on this flight: pushing thousands of pieces of tin foil called 'window' into a chute and out of the plane. These showed up on the German radar screens and played havoc with them.) Heading out over the North Sea into Holland, the bomber crews were about to encounter one of the worst electrical storms they were likely to come across. Outside, the temperature began to fall dramatically and the air became very turbulent, causing Zee's aircraft to become unstable. And while he was struggling to keep the plane in the air, it was being struck by lightning, with sparks flying everywhere, including the ends of the guns. The propellors resembled Catherine wheels. All the crew could do was hope they could ride out the storm. It was Zee's skill as a pilot and an element of luck that brought Harold home safely after such a terrifying experience.

On the evening of 17 August 1943, the usual briefing before an operation was somewhat different. First, Harold noticed that there were an unusually large number of military policemen around the camp. Secondly, when the crews were assembled, there was the unmistakable sound of the doors being locked. Clearly, something special was on. They were told that if tonight's target was not

Flight Lieutenant Swain, wearing his DFC ribbon and Pathfinder wings

destroyed, they would be going back again and again until it was. As one officer put it, 'We were told that our lives were not to be considered in the destruction of this target.'

The destination to which so much importance and secrecy was attached was Peenemünde, where the Germans were developing the V1 and V2 rockets. Harold was one of 4214 aircrew in 596 aircraft that crossed Holland on the way to the target. When they arrived, they were greeted by intensive flak. Zee's plane was one of the first to drop its markers and was then able to return home. The main force were not so lucky, because by now the sky was alive with night fighters, who had a field day among the bombers. One pilot said of that night, 'I had never seen such a sight before or since. All over the sky RAF planes were going down in flaming infernos.' 40 aircraft were lost, and 280 aircrew were killed.

By November 1943 Harold had been on 37 operations, but two changes came about that could affect his chances of surviving the war. First, Jerry Zee had now completed his tour and was transferred to the US Army Air Force, where he was to pilot Flying Fortresses against Japan until the end of the war.

The crew which had relied on each other for so many trips were split up and Harold would never fly with them again. The second factor was a change in bombing strategy. From now on, the main target was to be Germany's most well-defended city, Berlin. To add to the danger, the bombers were required to carry heavier payloads, which meant flying at a lower altitude and spending longer over the target. Also, the enemy had developed a new type of radar which discounted 'window' and allowed night fighters to assemble over Berlin and wait for the incoming bombers.

Harold flew six operations to Berlin in as many weeks, including one on 29 January 1944 which was to be his forty-fifth and last. Despite the odds he had survived. On leaving 7 Squadron he was immediately awarded the Distinguished Flying Cross and recommended for a commission, which eventually led to him becoming a Flight Lieutenant. With the commission came a new job, when he was appointed Adjutant of Signals at Corsewell, north of Stranraer.

As the war drew to a close, it was time for Harold to think about what career he would follow in Civvy Street. He decided to attend a prospective teaching course at Liverpool University, which ultimately led to him gaining a teaching post at Buckland Newton School, north of Dorchester. If his time in the RAF had been busy, life back home was equally so and he became a major figure in the community, despite being confined to a wheelchair due to polio. He was instrumental in the establishment of Dorchester Town Football Club and the Trinity Club and was often to be seen dashing round the town in a light blue Robin Reliant in his quest for used newspapers for charity. The importance of his voluntary work for Dorchester was recognised by the award of an MBE. His former employer, Mr Edwards, would surely have been proud of his clerk/typist.

Harold in his later years

The Last Rose of Summer

(A Dorset Memory)

The cottage had been long abandoned,
Its windows black and broken;
No spoken word is heard now,
No crackle of the fire, smoking.
Cobwebs adorn the chimney breast
And decorate every room,
No broom sweeps here now,
No fiddle plays its tune.
Once a home filled with laughter
Is now an empty space:
No trace of former days
When this home was a happy place.
Then, as I begin to walk away,
I notice a flash of red
Between the shed and aged door,
And as I move my head
I catch a beautiful scent
And, smiling, turn to see
The last rose of summer,
Planted years ago, for me.

Devina Symes

Ed Marriott

Andrew Headley has met a young Dorset artist with already an impressive past and with an exciting future

Ed Marriott painted this picture of Old Harry Rocks when he was only five years old

At the age of four, most children's artistic endeavours go no further than paintings labelled 'Mummy': orange splodges with lines for arms and legs. 'Prodigy' is an over-used word, but how else do you describe a child who in Reception class is producing paintings that not only are visually accurate but already reveal a sensitivity to the subtleties of colour? Such a child was Ed Marriott, who, now aged 20, is establishing a reputation as an exciting young artist who presents in a novel and thought-provoking way the Dorset scenes from which he draws his inspiration.

By the time Ed moved from London to Dorset with his parents at the age of four, taking over the top floor of his grandparents' substantial villa near the centre of Swanage, he was already drawing as soon as he woke up in the morning. It was not long before the family summer-house became his studio, and at the age of eight he was exhibiting his work, initially at Windjammers café in Swanage.

Although it may be a joy for parents to have a child with a particular talent, it is also a challenge to ensure that the talent is developed to its full potential while not neglecting the child's social

Elements of Ed's future style can be seen in this painting, which he did at the age of nine

and intellectual development. In Ed's case, it became clear as early as year 1 that conventional education was not going to work for him, so his parents took the courageous decision to home school him. His mother taught him the academic subjects, while his father, a carpenter by trade but with a keen interest in art, concentrated on the practical and artistic aspects of Ed's education. Ed was a musical child and, when not drawing, was usually teaching himself an instrument. He took guitar lessons every week with local teacher Mike Cahill and achieved grade 5. 'My parents encouraged me to go out to clubs

Each of Ed's paintings tends to be dominated by one colour, as in this view of Broad Street in Lyme Regis

nearly every evening,' recalls Ed, 'so I made as many friends as I would have done at school.'

Although Ed's progress was regularly monitored by the local authority, he took no formal exams, which could have posed a problem when it came to further education. However, he had built up a portfolio that was more eloquent than any exam certificate, and was accepted by Bournemouth & Poole College of Art & Design to do a course in fine art. For someone who had been developing a style, largely self-taught, for as long as Ed had, the course was not a perfect fit, and in his last year and a half he switched to graphic design, which complemented his style better. He graduated in 2022.

So what is this style that Ed has been developing since the age of eleven or earlier? Defining any artist's unique style is a challenge, but Ed's is characterised by strong outlines and judiciously placed blocks of colour. The result is almost architectural, but lifted by the vibrant colours. His basic colour palettes have been largely blue and green, which, against an uncompromisingly white background, give something of a Mediterranean air to many of his paintings. Recently, he has been developing more of a pastel palette and will no doubt

The blues are more muted in Ed's picture of
Swanage's Wellington Tower, which takes an
unusual approach to the subject in that the artist
is more interested in the foreground detail than
in including all of the tower

broaden his range further in the future.
Mastery of perspective is a feature of
his work, especially the street scenes, to
which, he says, 'I like to give the feeling
that they are leading somewhere.'

One's initial reaction on looking
at an Ed Marriott painting may be
that it is effective but fairly simple,
yet achieving simplicity is often a
complicated and skilled process. In this
case, the skill lies in arriving at just the
right amount of colour to give the work
strength while preserving its delicacy
and balance. For this reason, Ed uses no
more than five or six colours in any one
painting – 'Sometimes, less is more,'
he explains. The effectiveness of his
style can be seen in two pictures of an
almost identical view of Corfe Castle:
he uses different palettes and adds the
colour in different places, graphically
demonstrating how a scene can change
according to the season and the light.

Although Ed's inspiration is drawn
from landscapes and townscapes across
Dorset, especially in Purbeck, no
other artist or movement has been a
particular influence on him. He does
admit, however, to an enthusiasm for
railway posters, and one can see in his
style echoes of their blocks of strong
colour and bold typography.

Ed works in acrylic on canvas and
starts by painting the canvas white.
He then draws on paper the outlines,
which are transferred to the canvas via

charcoal paper. Sometimes he will take the sketch onto his computer and experiment with colours in Photoshop – a good example of how technology can serve and complement creativity without ever replacing it. The next stage is to fill in the blocks of colour, and only at the end are the strong black outlines added, using a pipette pen. This can be a temperamental tool and Ed's accuracy is remarkable, especially since the strong white of the background canvas is so important that if it is compromised in any way, he

sometimes has to go right back to the beginning and start all over again.

Ed's work is already represented in the Purbeck New Wave Gallery in Swanage, the Blue Lias Gallery in Lyme Regis, the Gallery on the Square (Poundbury), Seasons Green (Corfe Castle) and the Fossil Blue Gallery (Wimborne). He also produces cards via Art for Cards, based in Poundbury. His aim is to add five more galleries to this list in the near future and also to build on the commercial graphic design work that he has done in the past and enjoyed. That four-year-old prodigy is well on the way to becoming a significant contributor to the Dorset arts scene.

Above: Splashes of red set off the more muted green-greys and browns of this view up Swanage High Street

Right: Ed's growing interest in a more pastel palette is evident in this painting of Corfe Castle

The desperate affair at Scratchy Bottom

by Jack Sweet

The beach below Scratchy Bottom

The wonderfully named Scratchy Bottom is a valley to the west of Durdle Door and on the night of 28 June 1832 was the scene of a particularly violent encounter between the Lulworth smuggling gang and some local Preventative Officers.

During the late evening of 28 June, a coastguard from the Preventative Service station at West Lulworth was patrolling the cliffs to the west of Durdle Door when he saw a boat pushing off after landing barrels on the beach below Scratchy Bottom. By the time he reached the landing there were four men standing by the barrels and, suspecting a smuggling operation, he burned a blue lamp, the signal for assistance, and fired several shots from his pistol. The men made off and shortly afterwards, several fellow coastguards arrived at the same time as some 50 or so smugglers streamed down the valley. The gang attempted to seize the barrels and in doing so opened fire with muskets and pistols on the coastguards, who took cover under the cliff and returned fire. This went on for nearly an hour, without anyone being hurt, and on the arrival on the beach of Lieutenant Stocker RN and coastguards from the Osmington station, the smugglers withdrew back up the valley and dispersed.

In the meantime, Lieutenant Thomas Knight RN, the officer commanding the West Lulworth station, accompanied by Coastguard John Duke, was hurrying to answer the call for assistance when they were intercepted by some of the smuggling gang armed with long heavy sticks, who shouted that if the two men advanced another step they would be killed. Undaunted, the lieutenant and coastguard advanced and were immediately surrounded. Although they fired their pistols over their heads, the gang closed in. The two men fought back to back, wielding their cutlasses, but they were overpowered and beaten senseless. Thomas Knight was dragged to the edge of the nearby cliff and thrown over the hundred-foot drop.

Following the dispersal of the gang, the lieutenant was found still alive but badly injured at the foot of the cliff and despite the best medical assistance, he died the following evening. 42-year-old Lieutenant Thomas Knight left a wife and five children and was buried with full military honours in St Mary's Churchyard at Weymouth. Coastguard John Duke was reported to be battered and bruised 'to an alarming degree' but was recovering.

Just under a month later, on 26 July, John Davis and Charles Bascombe appeared before Mr Justice Patterson at the Dorset Summer Assizes at Dorchester indicted 'For having of 28 June at West Lulworth feloniously assembled with other persons unknown, armed with fire arms and other offensive weapons in order to and assist in the running and carrying away certain prohibited goods, namely 88 gallons of brandy, which are liable to pay certain duties to the customs.'

Despite the prosecution presenting a 'great deal of evidence' identifying the two prisoners as being present during the skirmish, Davis called five witnesses who swore under oath that on the night concerned he was in bed with a bad foot, and Bascombe produced four to testify that he was in bed at ten o'clock and stayed there until four the next morning when he went out to thatch a hayrick.

Each of the nine witnesses was subjected to very severe cross-examination by the prosecution but nothing could shake their testimony. After deliberating for some ten minutes, the jury found Davis and Bascombe not guilty and they were released. The killers of Thomas Knight were never found and it appears that there were no further prosecutions for the violent affray on 28 June 1832.

Looking down the valley of Scratchy Bottom

The George Albert Hotel

The perfect West Dorset venue for your dinner, meeting, exhibition or event

With capacity for up to 350 guests and over 600m² of event space

Easily accessible by national road network, situated on the A37 with free on-site parking

To discuss your requirements or to check availability please contact our events team

Call - **01935 483430**

Email - **events@gahotel.co.uk**

We look forward to hearing from you

The County Dinner 2023

The President addresses the dinner

The County Dinner was held this year on Saturday 29 April at the George Albert Hotel, Warden Hill. For many, the date was a departure from recent practice to hold it in October, but it was in reality a return to the original practice of holding it in the spring, Dorset Day being the first Monday of May. An immediate sign of the change was to sit down to eat while a beautiful sunset provided the backdrop, in contrast to the dark and often miserable conditions of a late autumn night.

The President, Lord Fellowes of West Stafford, was in the chair and members and guests numbering some ninety souls enjoyed an excellent meal, accompanied by the usual toasts and the ceremony of the cheese, this year being notable for the toast to the King after so many years of life with a Queen.

The guest speaker was Ken Tuffin BSc, who is the Managing Director of Pearce Seeds, a company which provides agronomy and agricultural services in Dorset and adjoining counties. Mike Pearce started the company in 1967 and was joined in 1986 by Ken Tuffin, and together they continued to grow the business. Ken spoke interestingly about the development of the company and the changes in agriculture that had taken place during its lifetime. Today Pearce Seeds is still run by the Tuffin family, who farm in the Blackmore Vale.

The President presented the Hambro Cup to Ray Davies, the winner of the annual golf competition, held at Came Down Golf Club in August 2022. A raffle was held and the proceeds donated to the Dorchester Food Bank. Lord Fellowes also gave his usual thoughtful and insightful reflections on the year just passed.

The Toastmaster was Alastair Chisholm, award-winning Town Crier of Dorchester and now also its Mayor, who made the announcements in his usual stentorian tones. The evening was organised by Chris Goodinge and thanks are due to him and his team for a most successful gathering.

Peter Lush

The unknown voluntary service

John Neimer gives the (mostly) official view of the
Independent Monitoring Boards

Every prison, remand centre or similar establishment has an Independent
Monitoring Board (IMB) which is charged with seeing that the establishment
is run in accordance with the rules laid down for it and that the prisoners are
treated humanely and fairly within the law and the rules of the establishment.
For ten years I was privileged to be a member of the IMB of HMP The Verne on
Portland, which is currently a Category C prison for sex offenders. Category C
indicates that the risk of prisoners attempting to escape is assessed as low.

Members of the IMB can visit the prison at any time (within reason) and
go anywhere in it (keeping in mind any security warnings that might be in force).
They take applications from prisoners who are unhappy about some aspect of
their incarceration and seek information about their cases from whichever part
of the prison is responsible, including the governor.

Boards are not part of the prison organisation and report directly to
the Ministry of Justice. They are made up of over a thousand unpaid volunteers
operating in every prison in England and Wales and every immigration detention
facility across the UK. Those volunteers are the eyes and ears of the public,
appointed by ministers to perform
the vital task of independent
monitoring of prisons and
immigration detention. The
IMBs' role is helping to resolve
even apparently minor issues
that impact directly on the daily
life and experience of prisoners
and detained people, where
everything they have, do or
need is controlled by others.
Apart from their observation of
individual prisoners, they also
report on whether prisoners are

The imposing main entrance to HMP The Verne

being given the support they need to turn their lives around. Boards can have a real impact on the lives of those held within these facilities.

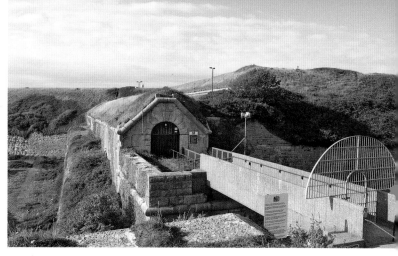

The previous back entrance to the prison from New Ground is no longer used

At regular meetings with prison and immigration detention managers, the systemic issues that arise from monitoring observations are discussed. This reflects back to managers what is actually happening, which may be different from what they hope or expect. The more accurate and evidence-based the reporting, the more likely it is to be acted on.

In carrying out their duties, IMBs sometimes uncover issues that can't be, or aren't, dealt with effectively by local managers. In extreme situations IMBs may go directly to the area prison group director, the director-general of prisons or the director of the Youth Custody Service. Or, in the case of an immigration detention facility, through the centre managers to the Home Office director of detention and escorting services.

Each board has a statutory duty to provide an annual report to either the Prisons Minister or the Immigration Minister. Boards can also contact the relevant minister at any time with important matters that affect individual establishments or national services as a whole, such as:

- potential breaches of human rights or statutory obligations
- resource issues that affect the whole service
- the impact of legislation or national policies
- the need for action by other departments, such as health or benefits.

The IMBs' work is part of public and parliamentary debate and that is why boards' annual reports, which are publicly available, are so important, highlighting both concerns and progress against previous recommendations. The national annual reports for prisons and immigration detention facilities collate the key themes raised in individual annual reports. There has been increasing media interest in IMBs' reports, drawing public attention to concerns that are being raised. IMBs also provide both written and oral evidence to parliamentary inquiries, drawing on published reports and real-time information collated from relevant boards.

So who are IMB members and what do they do? They:

- are ordinary members of the public
- are independent public appointees
- make two to three visits a month on average (but see below)
- monitor the day-to-day life and treatment of prisoners and detained people
- have unrestricted access to the facilities monitored
- can talk to prisoners or detained people out of sight and hearing of staff.

IMB members are unpaid, but it is a varied and rewarding role. Members talk to a prisoner or detained persons who are worried or vulnerable, who aren't able to access the support they need, or who need help to sort out practical problems. They get to see and report on everything that happens behind the walls: what day-to-day life is like, whether there is enough education and training to help with rehabilitation, what support there is for the most vulnerable, how physical and mental health needs are met.

You don't need qualifications to volunteer as a member of the IMB in a prison or immigration detention facility. Your values are more important. You need to be over 18, enthusiastic, open-minded and a natural communicator. You also need to be a good listener. In order to apply you will need to:

Inside HMP The Verne

-     commit to making around two to three visits a month
-     live within 30 miles (or a 45-minute journey) from the volunteering location, although this could be more in certain areas
-     declare potential conflicts of interest, for example any family connection with the prison or immigration detention facility

Would-be members should also be aware that prisons vary widely in form and function.

Most of what you have read comes from the official website. As with any system, once you are in it, the actuality is different; it doesn't say, for example, that an IMB member must be present if a prisoner is being subjected to forcible removal from a cell and must attend the subsequent wash-up meeting. Nor that members are expected to be present during parole assessment meetings, take part in drug detection exercises, check the quality of meals, assess the conditions of prisoners' accommodation and attend disciplinary hearings. On every visit, the duty member will go to the isolation block and speak to the inmates being held there pending removal or disciplinary hearings. The sick bay is also regularly visited. Then there are workshops where prisoners are (hopefully) doing constructive work and the education department, which in the Verne was a brilliant operation. We would also be present at the visitor centre when prisoners were being visited. The board would, if possible, be represented if there was an emergency of any sort for however long it lasted, for example a riot or other event affecting the prison.

As a board member I did all these things (except the riot) and was able to influence staff decisions by careful observation and informed comment. Of course, as I went around the prison premises, I would be stopped by prisoners where I could learn about their condition and, where appropriate, advise on a course of action to solve a problem. Members keep a journal in which they record their interactions with prisoners and the results of visits to parts of the prison. These journals are legal documents that might be used as evidence in an inquiry. Of course, all these duties are reflected in the number of visits required to cover them, especially if the board is not up to strength. Chairs of boards also attend the annual IMB conference which is usually a two- or three-day event.

Another part of the service with which we regularly liased was the chaplaincy. This was normally staffed by a chaplain responsible for several establishments and it was advantageous for him and the board to keep each other informed of prisoners' conditions and possible grievances. A similar contact was maintained with the visiting imam for Muslim prisoners. The faith leaders would be invited to attend board meetings to help in maintaining an amicable working relationship.

One thing a member will normally never do is ask why a prisoner is there although on one occasion, when a man was complaining to me at length about how violent he thought the staff were, I did ask him why he was in prison. After some shame-faced mumbling he said 'GBH'! On another occasion the relatives of a prisoner thought they would send him a birthday present by catapulting a present (a bag of cannabis) over the boundary wall. Unfortunately for him, they also included a birthday card!

Boards normally meet at monthly sessions to which the governor or another senior officer would be invited to give a report on their department. Prisoners' applications are discussed, experiences are shared, duties allocated, decisions regarding representations taken. Members who have attended meetings or operations in other establishments report their experiences and make recommendations. Wise governors always attend these meetings and are available to members as and when necessary.

Before closing, I should mention the Jailhouse café, which is the old officers' mess now staffed by prisoners as part of their rehabilitation and run as a functioning restaurant. It is located behind the prison, is open to the public and has a fabulous view of Portland Harbour and Weymouth Bay to St Aldhelm's Head.

Finally, I would say that in my time as a member of the board in the Verne, howimpressed I was by the care the officers and staff of the prison took in their efforts to help prisoners in their rehabilitation and care.

A member of an IMB listens to a prisoner's concerns

Arsenic in the Oxo

The late Roger Guttridge recalls a sad case that resulted in a hanging. But was justice done?

Charlotte McHugh, an unsophisticated Irish girl unable to read, write or tell the time, was 19 when she eloped with Frederick John Bryant, a military policeman serving in Londonderry with the Dorset Regiment. When he returned to Dorset and civilian life, they settled in a labourer's cottage at Nether Compton, near Sherborne.

Over the next dozen or so years, Charlotte Bryant lived in squalor with her husband and rapidly expanding family. She sought consolation by escaping to the local pub, by extravagant living, by taking a series of lovers. She built herself a reputation for accepting drinks from strange men and then disappearing with them afterwards. Some of them went back to her cottage and her children would be sent out to buy sweets.

Bryant was fully aware of his wife's reputation but tolerated it, even her relationship with the last and most serious of her lovers, Leonard Parsons. A wandering salesman and horse dealer with a taste for the opposite sex, Parsons became the dark-eyed Irishwoman's lover in 1933 and over the next two years spent as much time living at the Bryants' cottage as he spent elsewhere. Bryant

Nether Compton, where Fred and Charlotte Bryant first lived in Dorset after their whirlwind marriage in Ireland

Charlotte Bryant, née McHugh

not only tolerated the affair but became a close friend of Parsons. The two men often went drinking together at the 'Crown' pub and even shared the same razor back at the cottage.

Parsons was staying at the cottage on 13 May 1935 when Fred Bryant suffered the first of what was to become a series of mystery illnesses. He ate a lunch of meat, potatoes and peas left for him by his wife, but during the afternoon his next-door neighbour found him sitting on the stairs, groaning and shuddering. His doctor, Dr McCarthy, concluded that Bryant was suffering from some form of food poisoning and gave him a hypodermic injection. Mrs Bryant said he had eaten the same as the rest of the family, who had suffered no ill effects. This seemed to the doctor to rule out food poisoning as the cause of Bryant's illness.

Bryant made a full recovery, but on 6 August he again fell ill with diarrhoea and vomiting and again recovered. The illness was diagnosed by the doctor as gastro-enteritis. In October 1935, the family moved to Coombe, just north of Sherborne. Their new cottage was a bleak stone building and Charlotte Bryant soon became friendly with a near neighbour, Lucy Malvina Ostler, a widow with seven children and, like herself, illiterate. During this same period, Charlotte was losing her grip on the affections of Leonard Parsons and feared he was about to leave her.

On 10 December, while hauling stone in a quarry at the farm where he worked, Fred Bryant was suddenly doubled up by stomach pains. A few days later, a neighbour called Priddle was summoned to the cottage by little Lily Bryant and found the girl's father on his stomach, groaning and vomiting. Mrs Bryant appeared to be unconcerned by her husband's condition and Priddle phoned Dr McCarthy himself. Mrs Ostler was also called in to help nurse Bryant.

On 21 December, Dr McCarthy arranged to make up some medicine for Bryant, which his wife was to collect from Sherborne that afternoon. Mrs Bryant was away from the house for three hours. Bryant spent that night in bed alongside his wife, but with Mrs Ostler also in the room, bedded down on a cot. By morning his condition had worsened and the 39-year-old cowman died in the Yeatman Hospital, Sherborne, at 2.40 pm. Dr McCarthy was at his bedside, pondering over the cause of this mysterious and agonising death. It occurred to him that the symptoms were identical to those one would expect from arsenical poisoning. It was a possibility which had fleetingly crossed his mind at the time of the first illness in May. This time his suspicions were considerably stronger and he refused to issue a death certificate.

Most of the dead man's internal organs were packed into jars, sealed up and sent to the Home Office analyst, Dr Roche Lynch, for examination. His report confirmed that Frederick Bryant was indeed killed by arsenic. By this time the police had already checked the poison registers of every chemist's shop in the district. They had also visited Yeovil's glove factories, where red arsenic was readily available, being constantly used for the conversion of raw skins into leather. The police paid particular attention to an entry in the poison register of a Sherborne chemist, which recorded a poison purchase at the end of April 1935, a few days before Bryant was first taken ill.

Even more interesting was the recollection of a Yeovil pharmacist that on 21 December – the day Charlotte Bryant left the cottage for three hours to collect her husband's last bottle of medicine – a woman bought from him a tin of 'Eureka' weedkiller containing arsenic. The woman was unable to write, he said, and had signed her name with a cross. Mrs Bryant and Mrs Ostler, both now in custody as the two prime suspects, were put in an identity parade, but the Yeovil pharmacist was unable to pick out either as the woman who had bought weedkiller from him on the day before Fred Bryant died.

Mrs Ostler, however, made a statement that on the last night of Bryant's life, she awoke in his room at 3.00 am and heard Charlotte coaxing her husband to have a drink of Oxo. A few minutes later she heard the sounds of his vomiting and less than twelve hours later he died. This statement conflicted with Charlotte Bryant's version of events, namely that she was so 'fagged out' that she slept through the night, never stirring, much less waking to feed her husband Oxo.

Mrs Ostler also said in her statement that, soon after Bryant's death, his wife had pointed to a green tin in a cupboard and said, 'I must get rid of that.'

Mrs Ostler's description of the tin matched that of the tin of 'Eureka' weedkiller sold by the Yeovil pharmacist. A few days after Bryant's death, Mrs Ostler added, she was raking ashes under the Bryants' boiler when she found a burnt tin of the same size, which she threw onto the rubbish heap in the yard.

On 10 February 1936, Charlotte Bryant was charged with administering certain poison, to wit arsenic, to her husband, Frederick John Bryant, at Coombe, near Sherborne, and wilfully murdering him. The trial began at Dorchester on 27 May 1936. Vital evidence came from Dr Roche Lynch, the Home Office analyst, who claimed that ashes from the Bryants' grate were found to contain so abnormally large a proportion of arsenic that something containing the poison must have been burnt in the boiler fire. A burnt tin found in the yard had also contained arsenic, he said.

On the fourth and final day of a murder trial that had captured the attention of the nation, the jury retired at 1.30 pm to consider their verdict. They returned one hour later and the foreman announced that they had found the prisoner guilty. As the judge pronounced the inevitable death sentence, Charlotte Bryant let out a shuddering moan which broke the silence of the courtroom. Her piteous sobs could be heard long after she had disappeared from view.

The following week, Charlotte Bryant's leading counsel, Mr Casswell, received a letter from Professor William A Bone FRS, of the Imperial College of Science and Technology. The professor claimed that Dr Roche Lynch's evidence concerning the normal proportion of arsenic found in the ashes of domestic fires was seriously inaccurate. It had long been established, said Bone, that the normal arsenic content of house coal was not less than 140 to the million and was usually about 1000 to the million. Therefore the Bryant boiler ashes examined by Lynch contained almost the minimum proportion of arsenic (149 to the million) and substantially less than might be expected. This new information, far from corroborating Mrs Ostler's evidence as Lynch's erroneous statement had done, directly refuted it.

Casswell swiftly obtained a signed statement from Bone and served written notice of appeal, adding that in the interests of justice he would take the unusual step of asking the Court of Appeal to hear what the professor had to say. He could hardly believe his ears as the Lord Chief Justice, Lord Hewart, described the application as 'objectionable' and flatly refused to hear the professor, who was waiting in the corridor outside.

A day or two later, the Home Secretary, Sir John Simon, stated that both the appeal judges and the trial judge were of the opinion that the information offered by Professor Bone did not affect the validity of the jury's verdict in any way and that even if Dr Roche Lynch's evidence was inaccurate, the remaining evidence against Mrs Bryant was so strong that no miscarriage had occurred. 'And after most careful consideration,' added the Home Secretary, 'I have reached the same view.'

Once the hope of a successful appeal had been dashed, there was only one remaining straw for the 33-year-old Irishwoman to clutch at. She sent a telegram to the new king, Edward VIII. 'Mighty King,' it said, 'have pity on your lowly, afflicted subject. Don't let them kill me on Wednesday.' But the Home Secretary felt unable to advise the King to grant a reprieve and on 15 July 1936, Charlotte Bryant was hanged at Exeter Prison. Shortly before she died, Mrs Bryant made

The incriminating burnt tin of 'Eureka' weedkiller

a will in which she left 5s 8½d to be divided among her five children. Two days later her children were formally adopted by the Dorset Public Assistance Committee and the family split up.

Thus was enacted the final scene of a tragedy which had left two people dead and five children orphaned. It was also a tragedy which left several controversies raging in its wake. Not the least of these was the debate over the appeal hearing. Casswell was not the only member of the legal profession to feel that Mrs Bryant had been unjustly treated. In his memoirs, published 25 years later, Casswell remarked that he looked back on the Bryant case with 'special uneasiness'.

[The Bryant murder is one of the stories in *Dorset: Curious and Surprising* by Roger Guttridge, published by Halsgrove. ISBN: 9780857042972.]

FRANKS LTD
MAINTENANCE GROUP

Building repair & maintenance | Home refurbishments | Facilities management service

Serving all your interior & exterior maintenance needs

- Heating & Plumbing
- Boiler Installations
- Home Refurbishments
- Commercial Refurbishments
- Carpentry
- Kitchen Fitting
- Bathroom Fitting
- Wall/Floor Tiling
- Plastering
- Hard Landscaping
- Painting & Decorating
- Roof Repairs
- Electrical Installations
- Electrical Test & Inspections

01747 826656
info@franksgroup.co.uk
www.franksgroup.co.uk

Miss Louisa Seymour wheels the ceremonial barrow to the cutting of the first sod for the Salisbury-Yeovil section of the LSWR main line, while the spade is carried in front of her

Railway relics

David Lloyd takes us into a world of wheelbarrows

In 2016, *Dorset Life* published an article by me on Gillingham railway station to mark 160 years after the first sod was turned at Gillingham for the new link from Salisbury to Yeovil, as part of the plans of the London and South Western Railway (LSWR) to connect London with Exeter.

It was 3 April 1856 and a Sherborne journalist, Louis H Ruegg, was present and recorded the happenings of the day. To start with, the weather was awful and the wind whirled sheets of water onto heads, blew garments into ribbons and cast the speeches back into the faces of those who spoke. When the sodden field was left and the party sought some protection from the bitter elements under a large marquee, the water penetrated the canvas and found its way into the glasses of wine!

However, the ceremony still took place and the honour fell to Miss

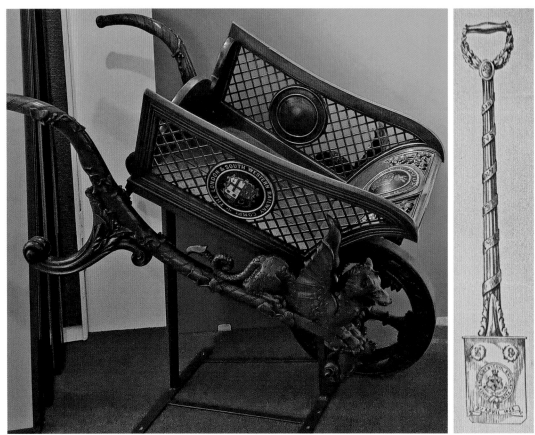

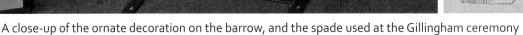

A close-up of the ornate decoration on the barrow, and the spade used at the Gillingham ceremony

Louisa Caroline Harcourt Seymour of East Knoyle to turn the first turf. Miss Seymour was the sister of Henry Danby Seymour, chairman of the Salisbury and Yeovil Railway Company and MP for Poole. A very elegant barrow and spade were prepared for the occasion. The barrow was formed of walnut, the shafts terminated in griffins' heads and the spokes were fashioned as sheaves of corn. It featured the arms of, among others, the LSWR, the Salisbury and Yeovil Railway Company and the Seymour family. The sides were of silver lattice work. The silver spade, beautifully engraved and ornamented, displayed the arms of the LSWR and the Salisbury and Yeovil Railway Company on one side and on the other an inscription stating that it was presented to the Hon. Miss Seymour on the occasion of turning the first turf.

My article continued with the development of the railway (the line was opened on 1 May 1859) and its beneficial effects on the development of Gillingham. Photos of the barrow and spade were published. Imagine my surprise when six years later, in 2022, I was contacted by Thorunn Lunde, a conservator at the Vest-Agder Museum, a union of eleven cultural heritage museums in the western part of the county of Agder in southern Norway. Thorunn contacted me because she had found my article on the internet and the Vest-Agder Museum holds one of three such wheelbarrows known in Norway. What details did I know about the barrow? Not a lot! – except that the barrow and spade were on display in Gillingham Museum. I needed to start researching.

I found an article in the *Dorset Year Book* of 1955, no less, which gave a bit more information about the items. The wheelbarrow and spade used in 1856 had been placed in the Corporation Museum at Yeovil. They were acquired by Gillingham Local History Society (formed in 1953) in exchange for a medieval form of prayer written in Latin on a strip of parchment for the use of dying inmates of Woborn's Almhouses, Yeovil. The barrow and spade were manufactured by Messrs Herring, Fleet Street, upholsterers to the Corporation of London.

I discovered that the Wiltshire and Swindon Archives held a copy of the 'Certificate of presentation to Miss Seymour 3 April 1856' and obtained a copy. This provided new information. The certificate stated, 'After the usual introductory remarks of the Chairman and other Gentlemen connected with the undertaking, the Chairman, H D Seymour, Esq. presented to his sister, Miss Seymour, the wheelbarrow. Mr Errington, in the name of Mr Locke, the Engineer-in-Chief, handed Miss Seymour the spade; and the Manager, R Norman, Esq., in the name of the Contractors, requested her acceptance of the gauntlets. After digging the turf, partially loading the barrow, and depositing the earth on the proposed Line, the Lady returned to the pavilion, where the Deputy-Chairman handed her the goblet filled with champagne, which she drank to the success of the Salisbury and Yeovil Railway. Mr Burt, in the name of the Contractors, delivered to the Lady a superb Purse, containing a complete set of Her Majesty's Maundy Money [in those days available to the public], being the first labour payment for work done.'

The wheelbarrow from the Vest-Agder Museum

I wonder what happened to the gauntlets, goblet and purse.

Science Museum

Two other examples from this country. Above: the Braemar station ceremonial wheelbarrow. Below: West Lancashire Railway 1873.

The gauntlets were composed of the finest French material, embroidered in gold and worked in blue, bearing the monograms of the Company and Miss Seymour, and the family motto, 'Foy pour devoir'(Fidelity unto duty) on the bracelet, which was fastened by gold tassels; they were made by Guibert of Paris. The goblet used by Miss Seymour to drink her champagne was similar in shape and size to the one manufactured for the use of the Empress of France when she visited the City, most exquisitely engraved, with the monogram and mottoes the same as the gloves. The purse, or wallet, was made of Russia leather, embossed in gold and confined by gold cords and tassels, and contained silver 1d, 2d, 3d, 4d and 6d coins of Her Majesty's new money. All these articles were got up from designs by Mr Burt and made under his immediate supervision.

By comparison, the wheelbarrow from the Vest-Agder Museum is much plainer than the one used at Gillingham. This oak barrow was used in 1891 for the start of the Setesdalsbanen. This 45-mile-long railway line, opened in 1896, linked the Setesdal to the coastal town of Kristiansand. With that town's port and connections to other Norwegian coastal towns and Europe, the line opened up a valley which until that time had been very isolated. There are similar barrows across the world and a few in the UK.

A newspaper cutting of November 1856 brings us closer to home. On 13 November, Lady Smith cut the first sod of earth in a ceremony at Blandford St Mary. Crowds of townspeople, school children and railway navvies followed a procession of horse-drawn vehicles from Blandford Town Hall to the designated area. Lady Smith was presented by the Dorset Central Railway engineer, Charles Gregory, with a ceremonial spade with which she dug a loosened turf and dropped it in the ornamental mahogany wheelbarrow, supplied by railway contractor Charles Waring. The Dorset Central Railway was to be short-lived, opening in 1860 and merging with the Somerset Central Railway two years later to form the Somerset and Dorset Joint Railway.

After the ceremony there was a grand lunch provided at the Blandford Assembly rooms. Henry Danby Seymour, MP for Poole and chairman of the Dorset Central Railway as well as the Salisbury and Yeovil Railway Company, addressed Lady Smith as follows: 'Lady Smith, allow me to present you with a glass of wine in which to drink success to the Dorset Central Railway. You have this day performed an important duty in turning the first sod of this great undertaking, which we hope through the blessing of God will be fraught with benefit both to agriculture and commerce, by connecting the Bristol and English Channels.' He also spoke of bringing clay to the new potteries in Poole and increased travel by passenger steamer to Cherbourg (and hence by rail to Paris) made possible via the railway line to Poole.

It's surprising what you find if you dig deep enough.

Blandford ceremonial wheelbarrow and spade, 1856

The author is Chairman of Gillingham Local History Society, whose committee govern the Gillingham Museum at Chantry Fields, Gillingham, Dorset. Hours of opening for Gillingham Museum can be found on the website www.gillinghammuseum.co.uk

100 years ago

John Travell has been looking at the *Dorset Year Book* for 1924

The 1924 *Year Book* begins with a poem in memory of the Society's first President, Sir Frederick Treves, by the Society's second President, Thomas Hardy. Treves had died in Lausanne on 7 December 1923, and his ashes had been brought home and interred in the Weymouth Avenue cemetery on 2 January 1924. Hardy's poem, 'In the Evening', had appeared first in *The Times*. The *Year Book*'s editor, Stanley Galpin, pays tribute to Treves in a leading article, for his 'taking the greatest interest in our Society' and for the many articles and photos Treves had contributed to the *Year Book*.

A 'Fascinating Lecture by Dr Cyril D May MA' had been given to the Society in London on 23 January 1923. This was a lantern slide lecture on the 50-million-year geology of the Dorset coast. The *Year Book* gives an account of Day's very detailed description of the many different geological features along the whole of the Dorset coast and of the variety of fossils that had been discovered.

The yearly dinner was held at the Holborn Restaurant on Dorset Day, 7 May 1923. The President, Capt. the Right Honourable Frederick E Guest CBE, DSO, welcomed 380 guests; those at the long top table included the Earl of Birkenhead PC, Col. Henry Guest MP, Viscount Chelmsford PC (the former Viceroy of India), the High Sheriff of Dorset (Major-General Sir J Pinney), Col. Sir Robert Williams and Mr H M Barton (Hon. Sec. of the Society of Yorkshiremen in London). The guest speakers were Lord Birkenhead and Viscount Chelmsford.

On 15 July 1923, Edward, Prince of Wales, came to Dorchester to visit his tenants of the Royal Manor of Fordington and to open the new Territoral Headquarters on the site of the old RHA Barracks in Poundbury Road. At the Drill Hall, Thomas Hardy was presented to the Prince. The Prince and Hardy then drove through Dorchester in an open-topped car to Max Gate for a private lunch, after which the Prince visited a number of his tenants and then Maiden Castle, Upwey Wishing Well and Weymouth, where he had tea in the Gloucester Hotel.

A long account of the Regiment, 'The Fighting Men of Dorset', reported that during training in Aldershot in May, the 1st Battalion had paraded before the King and Queen.

The Hardy Players once again came to perform for the Society in London, giving two performances in the King George's Hall at the Central YMCA of three one-act plays and a new play by Hardy, *The Famous Tragedy of the Queen of Cornwall*. This was not an adaptation of a novel but the first play Hardy had written directly to be performed by actors on stage, and it attracted full houses for each performance. A glowing review of the performances was specially written by 'London Critic', who said that, 'Good as their work had been, the Dorchester Players have not acted so well before as in Mr Hardy's new play.'

Thomas Hardy's wife was also in the audience, and at the tea following the matinée, the Society's Secretary thanked her for coming and asked her to 'take to Mr. Hardy their kindest good wishes'. Mrs Hardy was then told the story of a member of the Society who had been wounded and taken prisoner in the War. In the prison camp, a burly German sergeant spoke to him in English and asked him where he came from. Learning that it was Dorset, he asked him if he knew Thomas Hardy. The sergeant had all the works of Hardy in the camp and lent them to the prisoner. Mrs Hardy said she would like to meet the prisoner, who happened to be present, and Mr Arthur Cobb of Crichel, who had served in the London Regiment, was presented to her.

The Annual General Meeting was held in Caxton Hall on 26 November 1923. The Chairman of the Commitee, Mr J C Swinburne-Hanham, reported that the Society had 876 home members and 645 overseas members.

The *Year Book* had received full reports from 'The Darset Men Athirt th' Zeas'. It includes Wold Charl's annual letter in the Dorset dialect, telling the overseas members about the activities of the Society in London and Dorset. At their Annual General Meeting, the New South Wales Society were told that they had enjoyed their most successful year since they began. The NSW Society had over 200 members and expected this number to increase as they contacted more new arrivals from 'the old County'. Also in Australia, the Victorian Society 'had a highly successful dinner', with nearly 70 present.

'Interesting Letters From Overseas' received by William Watkins, praising the 1923 *Year Book*, came from Barbados, British Columbia, South Africa, New Zealand and Canada, where Watkins had travelled the previous year. Together with the names of all the members of the Society in London, the *Year Book* lists all the overseas members, in Argentina, Canada , Chili [sic], the United States of America, Uruguay, the West Indies, New Zealand, Egypt, South Africa and several other African states, Asia, India, Siam, Iraq, Singapore, France and Guernsey.

The 'In Memoriam' panel contains 24 names, including that of Sir Frederick Treves.

The Powys Society in 2022-23

A report from Chris Thomas, the society's Hon. Secretary

On October 8 2022 we celebrated the 150th anniversary of the birth of John Cowper Powys in Shirley, Derbyshire, which was his home from 1872 to 1879. JCP left a vivid account of his early childhood memories of Shirley in his *Autobiography* which we discussed in situ in his father's church of St Michael's in Shirley. During lunch at the local pub, the Saracen's Head, we raised a toast to JCP and afterwards walked a short distance up a narrow lane to visit the vicarage where JCP was born, pausing briefly in the garden to listen to readings from *Autobiography*.

In 2023 we commemorated the 60th anniversary of the death of JCP. On 28 June 2023 a memorial service was held at Radstock Museum and Ammerdown Centre to celebrate the life and achievements of Stephen Powys Marks, which was organised by his immediate family. Stephen was the eldest child and only son of A R Powys (younger brother of JCP). Stephen Powys Marks died on 8 June 2020. Stephen played a vital role in the Powys Society. He was past Treasurer of the Society, a member of the committee for many years and also responsible for the design of the Society's publications, which he produced to a high standard. Stephen was highly knowledgeable on all matters Powysian and an expert on Powys family history and genealogy.

Paris provided the setting for a special event in March 2023 when the bookshop, Halle Saint Pierre in Montmartre, organised an event to celebrate the publication in France of new translations of some of JCP's works as well as essay collections and translations of works by Llewelyn and T F Powys. Marcella Henderson-Peal, the Society's official representative in France, gave an illustrated presentation at the Paris event, explaining how the English and Welsh landscape inspired and influenced JCP's writing.

Our annual conference in 2023 was held from 18 to 20 August at the Hand Hotel in Llangollen, a short distance from JCP's home in Corwen. Members had the opportunity to visit places associated with JCP's Welsh novels – especially *Owen Glendower* and *Porius*. Lectures were presented on JCP and Wales, on his early novel set in East Anglia, *Rodmoor*, on Wordsworthian figures of disability in JCP's fiction, on JCP's eco-consciousness and on *A Glastonbury Romance* and the long modern novel.

Members of the Powys Society in Montacute, Somerset, for their 2022 conference

Volume XXXIII, 2023, of *The Powys Journal* was published in July 2023 and contains a variety of high-quality scholarly articles including a study of the Notebooks of Peter Powys Grey (JCP's nephew), a study of the place of Cronos in JCP's work, an examination of the relationship between JCP and William Blake, a study of JCP and Coleridge, excerpts from the diaries of Philippa Powys, the letters of JCP to our past President, Glen Cavaliero, and an essay on the recently restored chapters of *Wolf Solent*. This issue also includes two colour reproductions of paintings by Gertrude Powys.

Dawn Collins, our social media co-ordinator, arranged Facebook reading groups, which are always very popular with members and enable overseas members to join in discussions.

The annual gathering and meeting of the Dandelion Fellowship was held at the Sailor's Return in East Chaldon with a walk up to Chydyok to honour the birthday of Llewelyn Powys on 13 August. Our events calendar in 2023 concluded with a discussion of JCP's late masterpiece, *Porius*.

The Powys Society is a recognised charity and member of the Alliance of Literary Societies. The Society was founded in the late 1960s with the aim of promoting public education and recognition of the thought and contribution to the arts of the Powys family, particularly of John Cowper Powys, T F Powys and Llewelyn Powys. The Society publishes three newsletters and a scholarly journal each year. The Society produces other books by and about the Powyses and organises discussion meetings, on-line reading groups and an annual conference. The Powys Society is international, attracts scholars from around the world, and welcomes anyone interested in learning more about this very talented and unusual family. *www.powys-society.org.*

Obituaries

Trevor Vacher-Dean

Trevor was born in Poole in 1949 but had family roots in Milton Abbas and throughout his life was a proud man of Dorset. After leaving school in 1966 he joined the *Poole and Dorset Herald* as a staff reporter, chronicling all that was good or bad in Poole. He then joined the Devon Police having been unsuccessful with his application to join the Dorset Constabulary because he sported a beard! There he met and married his wife, Jill, and they eventually returned to the Bournemouth area, where Trevor had a successful estate agency business for some 20 years. They then moved back to Weymouth and he became the popular 'mine host' of the Boot Inn, which is the town's oldest public house.

Unfortunately, after four years or so, Trevor developed chronic obstructive pulmonary disease, caused by his exposure to passive smoking in the public house, and had to retire from the licensing trade. However, despite his medical problem he was able to travel extensively at home and abroad to visit their five children and twelve grandchildren.

Trevor joined the Society in 2003 and such was his great interest and enthusiasm for the Society that he became a member of the committee in 2006. He also reviewed books for our Newsletter with much detailed research and scholarly application. Then in 2013 he became the editor of the Dorset Year Book, but health problems meant that he reluctantly had to give up this post. Trevor was large of stature, gentle and affable by nature, but always good company.

Hayne Russell

Roger Guttridge

Roger died four years after his leukaemia diagnosis, an illness which he battled his illness with courage and determination right up until the end. He was well known throughout Dorset as a journalist, historian and author of over 20 books. He contributed to many publications, including the *Bournemouth Evening Echo*, whose district reporter in Wimborne he was in his younger days, *Dorset Life* and the *Blackmore Vale Magazine*. He also made many appearances on television and on radio. He was a long-standing member of the Society of Dorset Men.

He gave many hundreds of talks over the years, mainly about the connections between Dorset and Newfoundland as well as Dorset smugglers, the subject of his first published book. He was inspired by family tales of Roger Ridout, the right-hand man of Isaac Gulliver, a well-known smuggler.

Swimming was another major focus of his career, as a competitor and journalist, writing for the local press as well as the magazine *Swimming Times* and the national press. He was also Press Officer for the national swimming team for several years, travelling widely to cover various swimming events, including the Olympics.

As a writer, he knew that showing off with obscure words, long, convoluted sentences or a flashy style does nothing except put off the reader. His hallmark was simplicity: simple vocabulary and simple syntax. Simple, that is, from the reader's viewpoint – achieving that effect is for the writer anything but simple because it calls for a considerable talent and a lot of hard work.

For editors he was a dream contributor, never missing a deadline and always writing to his brief.

Throughout his career Roger was entrusted with the more sensitive stories, having built up a reputation for honesty and straightforwardness, a man who could be trusted.

John Newth

In Memoriam

The President and Members mourn the loss of the following worthy fellow Dorsets and tender sincere sympathy to their relatives.

GORDON AYERS (Weymouth)	Member	22/06/23
Mr R I BARTLETT (Child Okeford)	Life Member	08/06/23
JERRY BIRD (Dorchester)	Life Member	18/06/23
JOHN BROAD (Dorchester)	Member	19/04/23
HUBERT BEAVIS (Kingston/Corfe Castle)	Member	20/03/23
Colonel G J BRIERLEY (Charmouth)	Member	
LEN CARDY (Wareham)	Life Member	
RON COLEMAN (Dorchester)	Member	
GEORGE CUTLER (Weymouth)	Member	10/12/22
WILLIAM DAVIS-SELLICK (Weymouth)	Vice President	30/11/22
GERALD FOOKS (Thornford)	Life Member	25/04/23
BOB FOX (Upwey)	Member	05/01/23
DENZIL GODDARD	Life Member	
ROGER GUTTRIDGE (Sturminster Newton/Blandford/Wimborne)	Member	08/08/23
TONY HARRIS (Bourton)	Life Member	04/05/23
ERIC HOLDSWORTH (Wyke Regis)	Member	13/01/23
TERENCE HOLLAND	Vice President	17/11/21
JOHN HUMBY (Sherborne)	Member	30/12/23
CHRIS MARSH (Milton-on-Stour)	Life Member	12/08/23
GEORGE MOORE (Swanage)	Life Member	02/01/23
DAVID PILES (Weymouth)	Member	
JOHN PURCHASE (Wimborne)	Member	02/08/23
ROBERT ROBERTS	Life Member	
Mr G SMALLWOOD	Life Member	
DAVID SPACKMAN	Life Member	30/08/22
JOHN STANFORD (Swanage)	Member	04/01/23
GRAHAM STOCKWELL	Life Member	
DAVID TETT (Bridport)	Member	21/11/22
*TREVOR VACHER-DEAN (Poole)	Vice President	19/02/23
JAMES WAIGHT (Portland)	Vice President	17/06/23
DAVID WALTERS (Sturminster Newton)	Member	28/02/23

*Denotes past Committee Member

Rules of the Society

NAME

1.   The name of the Society shall be "THE SOCIETY OF DORSET MEN"

OBJECTS

2.   The objects of the Society shall be:-
To make and renew personal friendships and associations, to promote good fellowship among Dorset men wherever they may reside, to foster love of County and pride in its history and traditions and to assist by every means in its power, organisations of Dorset and individuals, who may stand in need of the influence and help of the Society.

MEMBERSHIP

3.   The Society shall consist of a President, Deputy Presidents, Honorary Life Members, Life Members and Members.

QUALIFICATIONS

Any person connected with the County of Dorset by birth, descent, marriage, property, past or present residence in the County shall be eligible to be elected to the membership.

MODE OF ELECTION AND TERMINATION OF MEMBERSHIP

5.   (i)   The names of all candidates for election shall be submitted to the Committee, who shall have full power to deal with the same.

(ii)   The Committee shall have the power to remove from the list, the name of any Member whose subscription is in arrears for two years.

(iii)   The Committee may also at any time in their discretion terminate the membership of any person without furnishing reasons for their action, in which event a pro rata proportion of the subscription will be returned.

SUBSCRIPTIONS

6.   The Subscriptions to the Society shall be (these subscriptions will apply whether the Member is residing in the UK or overseas):-

(a)   Life Member - one payment - £200.00.

(b)   Members per annum (payable 1st October) - £15.00.

OFFICERS

7.   (i)   The Officers of the Society shall be:-
Chairman, Deputy Chairman, Honorary Secretary, Honorary Membership
Secretary, Honorary Treasurer, Honorary Year Book Editor, Honorary
Newsletter Editor and they together with the President and Deputy
Presidents, if desired, shall be elected at the Annual General Meeting each
year.

(ii)   The Committee shall have the power to fill any vacancy of the above
Officers arising during the year.

COMMITTEE

8.   (i)   The Society shall be governed by a Committee consisting of the
Officers and additional Committee Members elected by the Annual
General Meeting. The Committee shall not exceed ten members
in total. Five Members shall form a quorum.

(ii)   The Committee may delegate any of their powers to a Sub-
Committee.

(iii)   The Committee shall retire annually, but shall be eligible for re-
election.

(iv)   The Committee shall have the power to fill any Committee vacancy
arising during the year.

ANNUAL GENERAL MEETINGS

9.   (i)   The Annual General Meeting will be held on a date to be decided
by the Committee normally in October.

(ii)   Not less than fourteen days before the Meeting, the Honorary
Secretary shall send to every member a Notice of the Meeting. The Notice
shall contain:-

1.   The date, time and place of the Meeting.

2.   The Agenda of the Meeting.

3.   Nominations, duly proposed and seconded, for Officers and
Members of the Committee.

4.   Any resolution by a Member, duly proposed and seconded, for
consideration at the Meeting.

(iii)   Any Member may propose or second one or more Officers for election to the Committee.

(iv)   Any Member may propose or second a Resolution for consideration at the Meeting.

(v)   Nominations or Resolutions must be submitted to the Honorary Secretary not less than twenty-one days prior to the Meeting.

(vi)   If the wording or subject of a Resolution is considered not in keeping with the aims and rules of the Society the Honorary Secretary, in consultation with the Chairman and Vice-Chairman of the Committee, will consider whether the Resolution shall be included on the Agenda or rejected. The decision of the Honorary Secretary shall be final.

SPECIAL GENERAL MEETINGS

10.   The Committee may at any time convene a Special General Meeting and shall do so within six weeks of the Honorary Secretary receiving a written requisition signed by twenty Members. This should state the subject or subjects to be discussed and the Resolution.   Notice of the date and place of all Special General Meetings shall be sent by the Honorary Secretary to each Member fourteen clear days prior to the date fixed and shall state the object or purpose for which such a Meeting is convened.

BOOKS AND RECORDS TO BE KEPT

11.   Proper Books of Accounts showing all income and expenditure   shall be kept by the Honorary Treasurer. The Honorary Secretary shall record and keep Minutes of all General Meetings, Special Meetings and Meetings of the Committee. The Membership Secretary shall record and maintain a list of Members under the provisions of the General Data Protection Regulations.

EXAMINATION OF ACCOUNTS

12.   At each Annual General Meeting two Examiners shall be elected to examine the Accounts of the Society for presentation to the Members at the next Annual General Meeting.

ALTERATION OF RULES

13.   These Rules may be amended, altered or varied by a majority of two thirds of the Members attending in person and voting at the Annual General Meeting or at a Special General Meeting.

Society contacts

COMMITTEE CHAIRMAN
See below*

OFFICERS
Hon. Secretary: Steve Newman
Lerret Cottage, 5 High Street, Weymouth DT4 9NZ
Tel: 07796 367693
Email: steveplov@yahoo.co.uk

Acting* Hon. Membership Secretary: Peter Lush
25 Maumbury Square, Dorchester DT1 1TY
Tel: 01305 260039
Email: membership@societyofdorsetmen.co.uk

Hon. Treasurer: Paul Newman
37 West Street, Bere Regis, Wareham BH20 7HJ
Tel: 01929 471891
Email: mogwich@hotmail.com

Acting* Hon. Editor, The Dorset Year Book: John Newth
18 Morden Road, Wareham, Dorset BH20 7AA
Tel: 01929 551852
Email: johnnewth@gmail.com

Hon. Newsletter Editor: See below*

MEMBERS OF COMMITTEE:
Douglas Beazer, Christopher Goodinge, Michael Kay, Alan Holley

Society Archivist and Historian: Rev. Dr John Travell
44 Cornwall Road, Dorchester DT1 1RY
Tel: (01305) 264681
Email: johntravell30@outlook.com

*The incumbent Chairman resigned at the AGM of the Society held on 8 October 2023, having announced his intention to do so after the nominations for election of officers had closed. It was agreed at the AGM that the committee would arrange for a Special General Meeting, including elections to any vacant or acting offices, to be held as soon as possible and in any case before the end of November. This edition of the *Dorset Year Book* went to press three days after the AGM, before specific arrangements had been confirmed. Any enquiries that would normally be addressed to one of the vacant offices should pro tem be addressed to the Hon. Secretary.